The Spiritual Life of Catholics

Proceedings of the Ninth Convention of the Fellowship of Catholic Scholars

September 26, 27, 28, 1986
New York, New York

Program Chairman
Fr. Kenneth Baker, S.J.

**Proceedings of the Ninth Convention
of the Fellowship of Catholic Scholars**

The Spiritual Life
of Catholics

edited by
Paul L. Williams

Introduction by John Cardinal Carberry

Northeast Books

A division of the Cultural Society of Northeastern Pennsylvania,
a non-profit corporation
Scranton, Pennsylvannia

The Spiritual Life of Catholics

Published with ecclesiastical approval

ISBN 0—937374—03—2

Library Congress Catalog Card Number

87-060-652

Cover Design by: *Bill Pilling*

Associate Editor: *Ron Semian*

Typeset by: *Mary Ellen Morgan*

Layout by: *Martin A. Devine*

Northeast Books Edition   1987
by special arrangement with the
Fellowship of Catholic Scholars

TABLE OF CONTENTS

Introduction
John Cardinal Carberry

It is a special joy for me to be with the Fellowship of Catholic Scholars at this, the tenth anniversary of the society. It is such a joy because, first of all, Saint Louis is the birthplace of the Fellowship. It was my privilege as the then Cardinal Archbishop of Saint Louis to host the first organizational meeting at Kenrick Seminary. As I reminisce about my years as Shepherd of the Church of Saint Louis, one of my greatest joys is that the Fellowship of Catholic Scholars was born in Saint Louis.

At that initial meeting, you were responding to the request of Cardinal Garronne for a strong voice of support for the teachings of the Magisterium. Fidelity to the Church and to the Vicar of Christ gave birth to this society and remains its very raison d'etre. I am sure that the Fellowship is a source of comfort and joy to the Holy Father, and to all who uphold the teaching authority of the successor of Peter.

Yet, in a certain sense, could it really be said that the very existence of a Fellowship of Catholic Scholars is something that would not be expected in the vibrant Catholic Church in the United States? Every Catholic scholar is bound to recognize the evangelical authority of Peter who has been given the charge to confirm his brethren in the faith (cf. Lk 22:32), to feed the lambs and the sheep of the flock of Christ (cf. Jn 21:15-17), and to be within the Christian community the primary witness of the Risen Lord (cf. Lk 24:34 - Jn 20:2-7). Without the successor of Peter as the guide and the supreme teacher within the Church, our reflections on our faith can only be classified as "the wayward spirituality of the individual," to employ the expression of Karl Rahner. Christian theology is essentially related to the Magisterium of the Church; to ignore that teaching office is to place oneself outside of authentic theology.

Yes, the Church needs the Fellowship of Catholic Scholars for it indicates that there are some who have strayed from authentic reflection on the Catholic faith and ignore the evangelical teaching role of Peter and his successors, In truth, the Fellowship is more needed today than when it held its first organizational meeting in Saint Louis some ten years ago.

For a decade now, you have stressed the important truth that adherence to the directives of the Holy See is intrinsic to Catholic scholarship, not only concerning matters defined *de fide*, but as the Second Vatican Council authoritatively taught in *Lumen Gentium, #25*: "This religious submission of will and mind must be shown in a special way to the authentic *Magisterium* of the Roman Pontiff even when he is not speaking *ex cathedra*. That is, it must be shown in such a way that his supreme *Magisterium* is acknowledged with reverence and the judgments made by him are sincerely adhered to, according to his manifest mind and will." This is the beautiful gift which the Lord has left to his Church so that the gates of hell shall never prevail against it (cf. Mt 16:18). Truly, the Church is the "pillar and ground of truth" (1 Tim 3:15).

His Eminence, Cardinal Ratzinger, also referring from *Lumen Gentium, #25*, quotes the following passage which is of great importance: "Whenever, they (the bishops), even though spread throughout the world but still maintaining the bond of communion between themselves and with the successor of Peter and authentically teaching on matters of faith or morals, are in agreement that a particular position ought to be held as definitive, then they are teaching the doctrine of Christ in an infallible manner."

In addition to quoting *Lumen Gentium, #25*, Cardinal Ratzinger adds the following: "Besides this, the Church does not build its life upon its infallible *Magisterium* alone but on the teaching of its authentic ordinary *Magisterium* as well."

There is no doubt that the Fellowship of Catholic Scholars is truly needed in the Church today. In you the authentic spirit of Vatican Council II is alive and your spirit gives encouragement and strength to others.

As justifiably proud as you should be of your past, even more determined must you be in your defense of the Church. More than ever, your scholarly studies, so powerful because so conformed to the *Magisterium*, are really and truly needed. I am certain that the Church can count on you. The first ten years have proven the need for the Fellowship of Catholic Scholars. For this reason, I am sure that you will play an even more important role in the Church in the years to come.

All in the Fellowship of Catholic Scholars place themselves under the protection of Our Lady, the Seat of Wisdom. They ask her to obtain the graces needed, especially in the trying times of these days to be with them and quide them in teaching the true authentic doctrine of her Divine Son, and of his Body, the Church.

May the Fellowship of Catholic Scholars continue its defense of authentic teaching as set forth in paragraph 25 of *Lumen Gentium*; may its numbers increase, and may the blessing of the Dear Lord be upon each and everyone of its members.

Trends in American Catholic Spirituality
by
Bishop Edward Egan

Identifying trends is a risky business at best. For trends are tendencies which can be intercepted by other tendencies and re-directed. More importantly, even the best of trend-identifiers are tempted to see things moving in the direction in which they would like them to go. Accordingly, I address the subject assigned me -- and invite you to address it as well -- keenly aware of the peril of the task.

All the same, permit me to note that I bring to this undertaking at least one rather unusual qualification. In December of 1972, I left the United States for an assignment in Italy. This was my third stint in the land of Dante and certainly the one in which I lived most intensely as an Italian, since none of my colleagues in the office in which I worked spoke a word of English, except for a Scot who died during my first year. Thus there stands before you a trend-identifier who appreciates the danger of his calling and who, in addition, is both foreign and domestic, that is, who left this land during the last year of Richard Nixon, returned during the fifth year of Ronald Reagan, and now dares to hope that his absence may have at least somewhat sharpened the objectivity of his vision. Whether he is more a Rip Van Winkle than an Alexis de Tocqueville, he must, of course, leave to your kind judgement.

* * * * * * * * * * *

In the past fifteen months I have noted three tendencies in Catholic spirituality in the United States which appear to me to be far and away the most significant. All three, I might add, came as a surprise.

First and foremost, I find that American Catholics in their thinking and talking about God, in the manner of their communicating with God at least in its externals, and in the style of life which appears to be resulting from both -- in a word, in their *spirituality* -- are seeking to re-emphasize a philosophical-theological approach, having become, it would seem, quite dissatisfied with the dialectic and presup-positions of modern psychology and sociology.

The tendency is evident on every side. Catholic bookstores are filling up with new editions and reprints of Augustine, Thomas Aquinas, and such classical spiritual writers as Teresa of Avila and John of the Cross. Adult education and campus ministry lectures, which ten years ago might have centered on the writings of Carl Rogers or John Kenneth Galbraith, now more often have to do with such issues as prayer in the Church of the Fathers or the *Spiritual Exercises* of Ignatius of Loyola. Even in the field of catechetics and religious education a change is clearly taking place. In the newest set of religious textbooks for the elementary school level to come to my attention, each three- or four-page section is summed up in formulae reminiscent of Scholastic language; and the summaries themselves are being printed in violet-colored squares the contents of which teachers are directed to have the students -- believe it or not -- memorize. Likewise, in successful seminaries, that is, in seminaries which are maintaining enrollment and moving their candidates toward the priesthood, Aristotelian-Thomistic philosophy is making a comeback along with class-notes in theology very similar in structure and style to the theology manuals of the thirties, forties, and fifties. Indeed, if you are invited to speak on visitor's night in a successful seminary and you wish to hold on to your audience, there is only one safe approach: take a clear Catholic position on just about anything, develop it with philosophical and theological precision, and illustrate the development with citations from Scripture, the Fathers, the classic theologians, and the encyclicals of the Popes. If, on the other hand, you are content to watch your audience quietly steal from the room, talk about Piaget or Erikson or report on the "data" recently gleaned from questionnaires sent to "x" number of carefully chosen house-wives. Philosophy and theology of a serious sort maintain attention; "with-it" psychology and sociology do not.

The same, moreover, holds true for conferences with Religious, discussions with the laity, and even sermons from the pulpit. You can read it in the eyes of your listeners. They have grown impatient with what not a few of them describe as psychological and sociological "meandering." They want substance, i.e., precise Catholic teaching in clear, logical and compelling language. What's more, they are prepared to leave you to your own devices if you are unwilling to meet their expectations.

Allied to this phenomenon is a desire for accuracy, especially in matters historical. This past year I attended a catechetical conference along with three or four thousand religious educators. One morning I settled into my seat to hear a familiar speaker for such gatherings. The theme was vaguely psychological; and, at a certain point, without explanation or preparation, the speaker announced: "If you want to know what popes and cardinals think of women, just listen to these words from Tertullian." I turned to a priest sitting next to me and inquired what Tertullian might have to do with popes and cardinals. "Who knows?" said he. "In these kinds of talks it's the spirit not the facts that count." In the afternoon I attended another presentation by another regular speaker at catechetical conventions. This one located the Council of Trent in what was described as the "Dark Ages" and put words of Irenaeus on the lips of Paul. I looked around. Some were amused. Some were annoyed. Many were slowly making their way to the back door of the hall. I decided to follow this last group and soon found myself in a large room, something like a gymnasium, where booksellers were showing their wares. The books were the kind mentioned above, the classics of philosophy and theology, along with re-editions of Scheeben, Guardini, Garrigou-Lagrange, Marmion, and the like. I had the feeling, and still have it, that the facts are indeed beginning to count as the era of "meandering" draws to a close.

Thus the first trend in American Catholic spirituality which I sense all around me is a trend away from the trendy. Catholics, who are concerned about things spiritual, are now demanding something solid, something tried, and, above all, something true. They are not eschewing the valid insights of serious psychology or serious sociology, but they will not be satisfied with less than serious psychology and sociology, or even with psychology and sociology alone. They want the object of their Faith to be articulated correctly, clearly, and fully. For this reason, they are focusing on serious philosophy, serious theology, and historical accuracy as well. This is what I believe my trend-identifying antennae are picking up.

The second tendency which I am perceiving on the selfsame antennae is a movement toward reinserting present-day Catholic spirituality in a Catholic tradition. Here I am using the word "tradition" in an historical rather than theological sense. From the latter half of the 1960's until recently, there was abroad a *feeling* (it hardly deserves to be called anything more) that in the nuclear era, the space era, the era of the Second Vatican Council, and all the rest, we must be prepared to "re-think" and "re-make" everything, confident that what will emerge will be superior to what is being replaced. Gregorian Chant, classic poliphony, and traditional hymnody, for example, were dismissed with something bordering on disdain. In a twinkling, it was expected, a new, "modern" musical expression would come forth. It did not, as one can hear everyday in our churches and chapels. Similarly, the Rules of Religious Orders and Congregations were announced to be out-of-date and accordingly set aside in many quarters with the understanding that appropriately selected committees would soon put together something better. They did not, as one can see everyday in our monasteries, convents, hospitals, and schools.

And so it went with perennial Catholic moral teaching and what was to replace and surpass it; with perennial Catholic manner of prayer and what was to replace and surpass it; with perennial Catholic parish structure and what was to replace and surpass it; with perennial Catholic discipline of the clergy and what was to replace and surpass it; with perennial Catholic lay organization and what was to replace and surpass it. The rejections of the old were easy. The "re-thinkings" and "re-makings" were not. It should therefore come as no surprise to anyone that Catholics who are concerned and serious about their spiritual life are now, as the psychologists and sociologists might express it, "looking for their roots."

Nor am I speaking here of a mindless flight from the present or a mindless plunge into the past. Much less do I have in mind the repudiation of everything that has come to the fore over the past twenty years for reasons more of the spleen than of the head. I am rather reporting a developing realization on the part of many thoughtful Catholics that we grow not by discarding what we were but by understanding it, being nurtured by it, and building on it. There are certain insights gained over the ages which should be passed on as a treasure to be cherished and enhanced. The same is true of certain time-honored practices, procedures, and customs. This is what I am persuaded Catholics are today coming to appreciate in large numbers and with extraordinary calm and conviction.

And where do I see signs of this trend? Frankly, everywhere. Retreat masters now suggest à Kempis, Thérèse of Lisieux, and even Chautard without apology. Parish missioners commonly advise daily Mass, holy hours, and family prayer in parishes which are thriving or coming alive. In faculties of religious education, courses such as "Patristic Prayer" and "The Spirituality of Francis de Sales" are supplanting "What Jung Has to Say to Christians" and "Radical Creeds of the Sixties," at least in the number of students in attendance.

Just a few weeks ago I was approached by a Sister who told me she had been involved in adult education throughout the late sixties and early seventies, until -- as she put it -- "there was nothing Catholic, or even religious, left in it." "And now, Bishop," she protested, "would you believe that I know of a parish which is starting a series on the spirituality of John Henry Newman and thinking about having another on prayer life in the early Church?" I replied I would believe it without difficulty, adding that I knew of a young people's group which is embarking upon a study of Benedictine liturgical piety.

The second trend then is *forward* into our history, *forward* into what was lived and loved before us and what can be lived and loved by us now, *forward* into our spiritual heritage.

The third and final trend is, for me, the most unexpected. I had been almost convinced by my European colleagues that American Catholics were in the process of losing their catholicity and turning themselves into a kind of national, even nationalistic, movement. The indications were impressive. In statements and documents of every sort we were reading of the "American Church" rather than the Catholic Church in America. Theologians and canonists were suggesting in articles and addresses that laws, principles, and institutions which may be appropriate for all other Catholics were somehow inappropriate for Catholics in the United States. Even some prominent members of the hierarchy appeared to be approving this overweening concern for the uniqueness of Catholicism in America.

No doubt there is still a good deal of this in the air. Nonetheless, I am happy to report that, at least in my judgement, it is waning. My reasons are as follows.

First, I am truly amazed at the large number of translations as opposed to original English publications which are to be found in Catholic bookstores, and, recently, I have been told by librarians both in seminaries and in Catholic colleges that the translations are curiously most in demand. Bouyer, Ratzinger, von Balthasar, Laurentin, Martini, de Lubac, Danielou, von Hillenbrand, Guissani, Maritain, and Gilson are just a few of the authors which spring to mind. Secondly, the number of young priests, religious, and laity who are seeking to pursue their advanced ecclesiastical studies abroad is skyrocketing. Ten years ago it was the accepted wisdom to remain in the United States so as to "plug into the unique American Catholic experience." Today the tendency is to seek the broader Catholic reality wherever it might be found; and, interestingly, extraordinary numbers are expecting to find it in Rome, where lodging for students is truly at a premium, as any diocesan chancellor or director of studies for a Religious Order or Congregation will be happy to report. Thirdly, language study is exploding in seminaries, in religious houses, and among lay groups committed to the Catholic apostolate. Much of this can be attributed to the need for better serving the burgeoning Hispanic, Haitian, and Oriental communities. This, however, does not account for increases on every side in the study of German, Italian, and, especially, Latin. Fourthly, among priests, religious, and informed laity, it is a commonplace to hear expressions of concern regarding the so-called "American Catholic morality," the so-called "American Catholic liturgy," the so-called "American Catholic Church." One evening a few months ago, after a graduation ceremony in a Catholic school of liturgical music, I was lectured by a young man about the danger and anomaly of pretending that the "one, true, worldwide Church of Jesus Christ" could somehow be reduced to a community of "self-important, self-sufficient, and self-satisfied Americans." I tried to plead my sympathy for the drift of the lecturer's remarks but was not given the opportunity. "Did you hear just American music tonight at Mass?" he inquired somewhat rhetorically. I confessed I had not. "And there is no reason why you should have," he added. "All things Catholic, and that includes Catholic prayer, must be open to the best and holiest wherever they may be found. Let's not forget, Bishop, that we are members of the *Catholic* Church, the Church Universal." I assured him I would forget nothing of what he had said and moved on to the next group in some strange way both chastened and delighted. A nationally oriented and limited Church would have little hope for survival, I told myself, with Catholics such as this one on the loose.

The trends, then, which I believe I intuit in Catholic life today are as follows: (1) a trend away from the merely psychological and sociological and toward the clearly philosophical and theological with an emphasis on historical accuracy, (2) a trend away from embracing every religious novelty that comes upon the scene and toward reconsidering and recapturing what is truly authentic from our Catholic past, and (3) a trend away from looking in on ourselves as *American* Catholics and toward broadening our horizon to include the entire Catholic world. If these, indeed, be the directions in which things Catholic are moving here in America, it is time for us to seize the day, encourage the movement, and rejoice.

* * * * * * * * * * *

Still, I would wish to add a footnote to my analysis and invitation, a footnote which at first blush may seem a bit esoteric but which I, at least, would consider quite relevant.

In the late 1300's, as the Middle Ages were drawing to a close, all of Europe became aware of a movement, not organized but widespread and crossing national boundaries, which in the Low Countries came to be known as the "devotio moderna." Pourrat describes it in the second volume of his excellent work, *Christian Spirituality* (Westminster, Md., 1953), as do Leclercq, Vandenbroucke, and Bouyer in the second volume of their even more excellent work, *The Spirituality of the Middle Ages* (New York, 1968) and Goodier in his *Introduction to the Study of Ascetical and Mystical Theology* (Milwaukee, n.d.).

The movement was above all a reaction to exaggerated intellectualism in the theology of the Middle Ages and exaggerated institutionalism in the dioceses, monasteries, and convents of the period. Not unexpectedly, therefore, its expression was anti-intellectual, anti-institutional, highly affective, popularly oriented, nationalistic, scientifically careless, and at times less than orthodox.

In the Low Countries it was championed by, among others, Gerhard Groote, a sometimes uncontrolled and always anti-speculative deacon who was clearly uncomfortable with existing monastic structures; by Florent Radewijns, an overly enthusiastic and politically contentious priest who shared many of Groote's positions regarding monasticism; and by Gerlach Peters, a purveyor of what historians like to term "an all but totally affective piety." In Germany its leaders were, among others. Meister Eckhart, a politically involved exponent of the German vernacular who tended to write like a pantheist; Heinrich Suso, the ebullient "minstrel of Germany," to borrow

Strauch's phrase, who was convinced that even in this life we are to become united with something described, perhaps with Dionysian intent, as the "Eternal Nothingness"; and Johann Tauler, a spellbinding preaching and poet who insisted that all souls are somehow divine. In France it had as its defenders, once more among other, Pierre d'Ailly, a Gallican nominalist; Robert Ciboule, a professor of theology who merchandised the doctrines of d'Ally to the Students of the University of Paris; and Jean de Cherlier de Gerson, a proponent of affective piety, the French vernacular, and the view that popes and bishops join with theologians and "those who discern the Spirit" in forming the Church's *magisterium*.

When exactly this movement of reaction began is somewhat disputed among authors. All, however, agree that it grew up virtually unnoticed more or less toward the close of the fourteenth century, spread rapidly, and simply evanesced early in the fifteenth century, leaving behind hardly a trace of its brief moment upon the European stage. Still in all, it was not without a message of value, to wit, the danger of over-intellectualizing and over-institutionalizing Catholicism and Catholic spirituality.

Surely there is something to be said for an expression of Catholic piety which is unencumbered by undue speculation and sustained by appropriate enthusiasm. Surely, too, there is something to be said for structuring the Church in many areas of its life without rules to cover every eventuality and with genuine openness to development at a human pace. The "devotio moderna" of the Low Countries, along with the parallel movements in Germany and France, was a witness to all of this at the turn of the fourteenth century; and it would seem to me quite fair to say something very similar about what has been transpiring in the Church of Jesus Christ over the past two decades of this century, especially here in the United States of America.

If so, we would be well-advised to emulate our forebearers of the fifteenth century, many of whom, largely because of the "devotio moderna" type phenomena, learned to balance their concern for matters of the head with a concomitant concern for matters of the heart, and to temper their desire for order in Church institutions with compassion for the individual and his or her human needs. Allow me, to express the same idea in another way. If we are indeed witnessing the beginning of the end of a kind of second "devotio moderna," as I would suggest we are, it might be wise to keep in mind that the reaction to which the Church has been recently subjected was very likely due, in part, to exaggerations that needed to be attended to thirty or forty years ago and that need now to be identified in order to be avoided in the future. In addition, as the reaction wanes, I would hope that we will not allow its valid and valuable insights and gains to slip away with it. The theologies of Groote, Radewijns, and Peters, for instance, probably have little to recommend them and richly merit to be forgotten in the libraries of Holland and Belgium. Nonetheless, among their confreres in the "devotio moderna," there was a humble novice master and copyist of the Monastery of Zwolle who left behind a treasure which perhaps all of us here have read and which, one hopes, many generations after us will continue to read. I refer, of course, to Thomas Hermerken à Kempis, the author of the *Imitation of Christ*.

The reaction of the past twenty years, I dare again to suggest, is finishing its course; and it is well that it is. There are, however, reasons for why this reaction happened which need to be meditated; and there are too products of it which deserve to be preserved. Certainly this is no time for gloating or crying victory. Rather, it is time for identifying the healthy, promising trends of this new era of ours and seeking to support and promote them. If we assume this tactic, it may be that the "renewal and reform" of which the Fathers of the Second Vatican Council spoke (cf. *Unitatis redintegratio*, n. 4) is within our reach now as never before.

Spirituality and the Sacramental Life of the Church
by
Fr. Thomas Weinandy, O.F.M. Cap.

The Foundational Principles

"Christ has died. Christ is risen. Christ will come again." This threefold Eucharistic proclamation represents the heart of Christian spirituality as well as the purpose of the sacraments within the Church's life. First, through the death of Jesus the power of sin has been broken and the kingdom of Satan has been destroyed. No longer need humanity suffer under the yoke of Satan and the slavery to sin and death. Secondly, through his bodily resurrection Jesus reigns glorious as Lord of all creation. Sitting at the Father's right hand, he is authorized to pour forth his Spirit upon the world. Through faith in Christ, we can be transformed into new creations sharing in a new relationship with the Father through the indwelling Spirit. Thirdly, Jesus now awaits the time when all his enemies will be placed under his feet, and all who share in his new life will be raised with him to the glory of heaven.

Christian spirituality, by definition, is a sharing in the transforming power of Jesus' death and resurrection and the subsequent yearning to be with Christ in glory. It is the role of the sacraments to make present these saving actions of Christ in specific ways. These sacramental actions cleanse and heal; they sanctify and empower; and they anticipate their fulfillment in heaven.

The Contemporary Crisis

Today there is a crisis within spirituality and as a result in the sacramental life of the Church due precisely to the ignorance and absence of these fundamental truths. Much, if not most, contemporary spirituality and liturgical practice is founded upon grounds other than the reality of sin, the sacrificial and atoning death of Jesus, and the radical transforming power of his resurrection. Neither is there clear evidence that both the Cross and resurrection point to and foster an eternal life that exceeds this world and its concerns.

Contemporary spirituality (and its expression within the sacraments) is often predicated upon a sentimental notion of God's love and his tolerance and acceptance of human mistakes. Hence, it is founded upon a naive optimism that human beings are basically good and sincere. The presumption is that a majority of people appear to try hard to do what is right, as judged subjectively by their conscience. Christian spirituality, then, is understood as the process by which we are able to participate in this universal, non-judgmental offer of God's love and be unconditionally affirmed in one's person, strengths and weaknesses combined, and in one's life style, whatever it may be. The sacraments become "sacred" actions which aid this process in which the body of believers makes present this embracing unconditional love of God through their own non-judgmental affection and affirmation of one another. In such "sacramental" actions they are making present, through words and actions, the example of Jesus who was the fullest expression of the Father's mind and attitude toward humanity. The end purpose of such a spirituality and sacramental practice is not to prepare one for a new and glorious life after death, but to promote psychological well-being and self-fulfillment in this life and a better, more caring world. This is not meant to be a caricature but rather a summary of the defective theology underlying much contemporary spirituality and sacramental theology.

Obviously this position does contain "bits" of the truth. However, because these legitimate aspects of contemporary spirituality are not linked with the whole of Christian doctrine, they become grossly deceptive and false, as the example of God's love illustrates. God does love us even when we sin, *but* if we sin gravely we cut ourselves off from that love, and until we repent, we stand condemned. To separate the doctrine of God's love from the realtiy of freedom and sin is to distort severely the true nature of God's love, that he loves truth and good and not evil. If God did tolerate sin and evil, as much as contemporary spirituality seems to presume, he would not be more "lovable," but actually a hideous affirmer of massive injustice and wrong. Moreover, to pretend that sins are but the unintentional mistakes of sincere people, or the idiosyncrasies of the psychologically immature, does not enhance the dignity of men and women but radically undermines human intelligence, freedom and virtue. Saintly virtue and character are only possible when you are faced with the real choice of doing something that you know to be evil and yet which seems self-fulfilling. Saints are born from the struggle of fighting sin and striving to do good by the power of the Spirit. To lessen the struggle is neither caring nor helpful; instead, it devastates humanity's true calling to become as holy and as perfect as God.

There is another contemporary phenomenon that has filtered into Christian spirituality and contributed to the present crisis, an attitude that we might call spiritual Consumerism. Contemporary Consumer culture nurtures the idea that everyone is allowed to and has the right to choose the product that suits him or her the best. Industries cater to and promote this "right" by providing many options to choose from. All of the products, ranging from soaps to cars, center upon enhancing oneself and furthering one's own fulfillment. This consumerist mentality has infected Christian spirituality: we are offered a variety of spiritualities, some of which can be termed traditional, such as Franciscan, Ignatian and Carmelite, and others that are contemporary, such as Creation Spirituality, Wholeness spirituality, and Feminist Spirituality. We are allowed, even encouraged, to choose the spirituality that suit us best. As with secular consumerism, this spiritual consumerism is aimed at individual self-fulfillment, at what best seems to enhance our personality and spiritual well-being.

However, the Church today needs the simple truth of the Gospel itself more than any one spirituality. (I will develop this point shortly). The plethora of spiritualities, molded and tailored to suit the whims and fancies of every individual, has enfeebled the power and life of the Gospel by focusing on one aspect of that Gospel and ignoring the whole, thus distorting that one truth in the process. This is central to understanding the present crisis. For example, in creation spirituality, where the goodness of creation is emphasized, the whole reality of personal sin and repentance, with the need for redemption, becomes minimized. This in turn jeopardizes the goodness of creation, since it is obvious that there is sin and evil in the world. Yet, within creation spirituality there is no redemptive principle available by which sin and evil can be overcome and by which persons can be recreated and made new. Any creation spirituality that downplays the fall and redemption cannot stand the test of reality.

This contemporary emphasis on "spiritualities" has also jeopardized the true nature of the classic spiritualities, which are not spiritualities in the modern sense. St. Francis did not preach a Franciscan spirituality, but what he believed was at the heart of the Gospel: repentance from sin and new life in Jesus Christ, the crucified Savior. St. Ignatius of Loyola did not believe his *Exercises* were a new spirituality. Rather, the *Exercises* were his anointed means to lead people to a deep and ongoing conversion. Those who undertook the *Exercises* were led to forsake the kingdom of Satan, sin and the world and to choose wholeheartedly the Kingdom of God personified in the Lord Jesus. John of the Cross and Teresa of Avila did not propose a Carmelite alternative to the Christian life; what they called for was a dramatic return to the Gospel.

The sacred liturgy itself redresses the wrong done by this contemporary smorgasbord approach to spirituality, for it embodies the whole of the Gospel necessary for any mature spirituality. It begins with the goodness of God's initial creation, and moves from the fall through the incarnation, redemption, and Pentecost to the Second Coming. Each Sacrament, and the Liturgical year as a whole, presents the fullness of the Gospel reality. Every Catholic in each sacrament, and through the liturgical year, participates in all the truths of the Gospel; we cannot pick and choose. Thus the sacramentality of the Church fosters a true Christian spirituality that embraces the whole Gospel and protects the Church against spiritualities which embody only a few preferred themes.

Having stated the foundational principles of Christian spirituality as the death and resurrection and second coming of Jesus, and having briefly illustrated how contemporary spirituality is not based upon these truths, I would like to discuss these truths further and demonstrate how both Christian spirituality and the Church's sacramental life are founded upon them.

The Fall

A clear understanding of the Fall and its effects is the first foundational element in any true Christian spirituality and in sacramental life. Not only do today's spiritual writers show little interest in the Fall and sin, but even among the general Catholic population, laity and clergy alike, there is often no clear consciousness of either of these realities.

While God did create all things good, and while humanity and all creation were in perfect harmony with him, our first parents rebelled against the goodness, authority and justice of God. Adam and Eve attempted to usurp the authority of God, making themselves gods (see Genesis 3). This original sin, inherited by each descendant who ratifies it as their own, in his or her sinful actions, is an infinite affront to the very justice and holiness of God and is an insult to the boundless and constant love that God has for us. This sin literally made us enemies of God. St. Paul is adamant that "None is righteous, no, not one; no one understands, no one seeks for God. All have turned aside, together they have gone wrong; no one does good, not even one." (Romans 3:11-12; see Psalm 14:1). Only in the light of Jesus' death and resurrection can we recognize the full extent of the injustice done to God and the devastating effect sin has had on our own personalities. So great was this injustice that only the offering of the life of God's incarnate Son could make adequate reparation. Human beings were so enslaved to sin and Satan that only the Son could break the bonds of these evil powers. Man's situation before God, prior to the salvation offered through Christ, is not a positive one that only needs to be revealed or made better, as some contemporary theologians propose. Rather, what Jesus reveals is that apart from him and the salvation he brings, our relationship to God is absolutely broken. We are unable to know God personally; we cannot experience his intimate love as a Father. His Spirit does not dwell in us. Neither can we live by the Spirit's power. As Paul knew well, we are ruled by our passions to such a degree that we do not do the good we desire, but the very evil we know to be wrong (see Romans 7:19). Moreover, our relationships with others are scarred by bitterness, resentment and hate. We have become children of Satan; we are slaves to sin; we are at enmity with God (see John 8:44; Galatians 4:3; Romans 5:10). Without the salavation of Jesus all of us would deserve nothing less than eternal damnation. This is neither exaggerated rhetoric nor language which needs to be demythologized; it is the truth that God has revealed to us about our desparate need for healing and redemption.

To know within ourselves every day the depth of our fallen nature and the tight hold that sin has upon us is the first and constant truth upon which a Christian spirituality is built and nurtured.

Likewise the true nature of the sacraments as the forgiving, healing and redeeming actions of Christ will never be appreciated without a clear awareness of sin and God's judgement against it. Jesus noted that the first thing the Spirit does upon arrival is convict of sin (John 16:8). All of the saints were keenly aware of their own sinfulness as they stood before the holiness and justice of God. Significantly all of the sacraments not only contain within them the recognition of sin and the need for repentance and forgiveness, but they also make present the redemptive action of Christ.

The Incarnation

The second foundational principle of a true Christian spirituality and sacramental life is Jesus and his cross and resurrection. Christian spirituality is by definition centered upon the person of Christ and his saving death. According to John, the Father sent his Son into the world not to condemn us, but that we might find salvation in him (see John 3:16-17; 1 John 4:9). As the Incarnate Son of God, Jesus is the Father's solution to the problem of humanity's slavery to sin, death and Satan. The eternal Son came into the world in order to change our relationship with the Father, enabling us to become his sons and daughters. An inspired prophet or some wise philosopher could proclaim some religious "truth," but only God can actually make up for the infinite injustice done to him by sin; only he can destroy the powers of Satan which are beyond man's control and which enslave him. Only God can establish an entirely new kind of relationship between himself and his creation. The traditional doctrine of the Incarnation, that Jesus is God the Son existing as man, is absolutely essential for accomplishing the work of salvation that needs to be done.

The Cross

The cross and resurrection are the heart of Jesus' work of redemption. It was for this very reason that he came into the world. Thus, the mystery of Jesus' death and resurrection must be the center of Christian spirituality and the Church's sacramental life. In the Eucharist we pray: "Father, we celebrate the memory of Christ, your Son. We, your people and your ministers, recall his passion, his resurrection from the dead and his ascension into glory." This is "the holy and perfect sacrifice; the bread of life and the cup of eternal salvation" (*Roman Canon*). How does this paschal mystery change the life of a person and become the source of spiritual growth?

Paul emphatically declared to the Corinthians that the cross is complete absurdity for those headed for ruin, but "to us experiencing salvation it is the power of God" (1 Corinthians 1:18). Too often today the cross is seen merely as the good example of Jesus, that he was willing to die for those he loved. In our turn, we, too, must sacrifice ourselves for one another. In a similar vein, popular Catholic tradition saw Jesus' exhortation for us to take up our cross daily and follow him to mean that we must bear up under persecution, burdens, temptations and sickness. These are the crosses we must bear. Obviously these thoughts contain some truth, but they fail to do justice to the more central truth that the cross is the power of God. It is the power of the cross that is the source of a Christian life and what is mediated through the sacraments.

The Cross: God's Justice

How is the cross the salvific power of God in the life of the believer? First, the cross of Jesus is God's justice so that we might be just. In the Preface for the *Passion of the Lord* we pray: "The power of the cross reveals your judgement on the world and the kingship of Christ crucified." The cross pronounces judgement against sin and offers new holiness in Christ.

Man's sin is primarily an arrogant affront to the very holiness, sovereignty and justice of God. Jesus, in offering himself to the Almighty Father out of total love and in reparation for the sin of the world, rectified the infinite wrong done to God. Prior to Jesus' sacrificial and atoning death we were "powerless" and "godless men" (see Romans 5:6-8).

The cross of Jesus radically changes our situation and status before God. "All men are now undeservedly justified by the gift of God, through the redemption wrought in Christ Jesus" (Romans 3:23). "It is in Christ and through his blood that we have been redeemed and our sins forgiven" (Ephesians 1:7). We have been "justified by his blood" and "saved by him from God's wrath" (Romans 5:9). We who were strangers and aliens have been reconciled to the Father (Colossians 1:21). "We are at peace with God through Our Lord Jesus Christ" (Romans 5:1). "We have been sanctified through the offering of the body of Jesus Christ once for all" (Hebrews 10:10).

The basic truth of these passages is that the cross of Jesus is the vehicle by which we have access to the Father once more, for by the death of Jesus, God's justice is restored and humanity is cleansed of the sin that had condemned us before the throne of God. In offering his life as a sacrifice of atoning love to the Father, "Christ was offered up once for all to take away the sins of many" (Hebrews 9:28). The blood of Christ, as an offering to the Father of the eternal Son, has washed us clean of sin and guilt. He has enabled us once more to stand justified and holy before the Father.

We see here the primary aspect of the cross' power. When a person repents of sin and believes in Jesus, either at the moment of conversion or subsequently in daily prayer, he is reconciled to the Father through the cross of Jesus. No longer is the person justly accused and condemned because of the infinite wrong done to the love and justice of God. Rather, the believer lays hold of the cross and its benefits by which he or she is cleansed of sin, freed from condemnation, justified and made holy. "By his dying he destroyed our sins, by his rising he has raised us up to holiness of life" (*Preface: Passion Sunday*). The power of Jesus' death allows the believer to have access once more to the Father and to receive the love of the Father "poured out in our hearts through the Holy Spirit" (Romans 5:5).

Contemporary spirituality and sacramental theology is oblivious for the most part to this fundamental truth. Yet this is the primary source of a Christian's spiritual life. Uniting oneself to the atoning death of Jesus allows one to have an entirely new relationship with God in the Spirit which begins a process of healing from sin and growth in holiness and justice. All Christian prayer and the sacraments find their efficacy in the cross of Jesus. Devotion to the Sacred Heart is an excellent illustration. All grace and blessings flow from the side of Christ (Spirit and life) precisely because Jesus offered himself to the Father in loving reparation for sin and out of love for us who stood condemned. All praise, adoration and thanksgiving to Jesus resides in the truth that only by his cross is sin forgiven and peace with the Father restored.

The Mass as Sacrifice

This cornerstone of Christian spirituality finds its greatest expression in the sacrifice of the Mass. Recent sacramental theology has stressed the banquet and communal aspects of the Eucharist. This is necessary and right. However, the Eucharist is a communal meal only because Jesus has shed his blood. In this he cleansed us of sin and reconciled us to the Father and to one another. In the Mass, the very sacrifice of Jesus on the cross is made present to all generations so that each person might be united to this one atoning offering to the Father. Together with Christ, the priest and victim, those who participate in the Eucharist offer themselves in thanksgiving and praise to the Father in reparation for their sins and in turn receive the cleansing, healing and sanctifying benefits of Jesus' sacrifice. We "see the Victim whose death has reconciled us to" the Father. We are "nourished by his body and blood" and are "filled with his Holy Spirit" (*Eucharistic Prayer III*). The Mass is the pinnacle and summit of the transforming work of the cross in our midst, for through it God's people are freed from sin and death and receive in communion the heavenly life of Jesus' risen body and blood making them holy and just. This is in anticipation of the heavenly banquet when we will be fully joined to the risen Lord in offering praise and adoration to God the Father.

The Cross: Putting to Death the Old Nature

There is another very important work of the cross that bears upon our spiritual and sacramental life. Through the cross of Jesus our fallen humanity is put to death and a risen, glorious new humanity comes into being. When Jesus became man he took upon himself a fallen nature subject to all the effects of sin: temptation, sickness, suffering and death (see Hebrews 2:14-18; Romans 8:3). Even though he did not sin, he was not immune to its reality, but was subject to the most brutal attacks of Satan and his fellow men. The cross itself is the conquering of the hatred, jealousy and rage that was heaped upon him.

Now, when Jesus died on the cross, that fallen human nature died with him. When he rose, he rose as a glorious human being no longer subject to the effects of sin and death. No longer could Satan have power against him. He was a new creation, a new Adam, the first-born of many brothers and sisters (see Romans 8:29). Through repentance, faith and baptism, a person comes to share in this new humanity, this new creation, this new life of God's Spirit. The Christian believer participates in a whole new reality within his or her life. The Christian belongs to a new race of people, those transformed by the cross and resurrection of Christ. This transformation begins with baptism and conversion and should continue throughout the person's entire life only to be completed in one's own glorious resurrection at the end of the world. This, too, is the heart of Christian spirituality and sacramental practice. Each day a person, through prayer, repentance, participation in the sacraments, and keeping God's commands, is fostering this transformation. In these actions, he or she is daily putting to death the old nature through the cross of Christ and bringing to life the new nature, the glorious life of Jesus' risen Spirit.

Paul clearly articulates this spiritual transformation as central to Christian life and sacramental practice: "Are you not aware that we who were baptised into Christ Jesus were baptized into his death?" (Romans 6:3). The power of Jesus' cross puts to death not only his fallen nature but those who are united to him as well. "Our old self was crucified with him so that the sinful body might be destroyed and we might be slaves to sin no longer" (Romans 6:6). This is extremely important not only for understanding the nature of Christian baptism but also for one's whole subsequent spiritual life. In baptism and in our daily Christian life the power of the cross is present, not just as an example, but by actually putting to death the sin which reigns within us. To take up our cross as Jesus commands is primarily to put to death our sinful nature every day, and not just to carry the burden of problems and suffering. This power of the cross is exercised by the new life in the Spirit dwelling within us. "If we have been united with him through likeness in his death, so shall we be through a like resurrection" (Romans 6:5). The radical transformation is beautifully expressed in the prayer of exorcism in the *Rite of Baptism*: "Almighty and ever-living God, you sent your only Son into the world to cast out the power of Satan, the Spirit to rescue man from the kingdom of darkness, and bring him into the splendor of your kingdom of light... Set him free from original sin, make him a temple of your glory, and send your Holy Spirit to dwell in him." The Christian through faith and baptism lives an entirely new life in Christ, a life in which sin is put to death and holiness of life is fostered through the indwelling Spirit (see Romans 6:8, 11, 23).

Putting on the Mind of Christ

Most contemporary Catholics are completely ignorant of the transforming work of the cross of Christ in baptism and in the Christian life, and they are unaware of the uniquely Christian effects that flow from it. First, participating in the glorious humanity of Christ, the Christian receives the Spirit by which he or she becomes an adopted son or daughter and has the right and privilege of calling God "Abba," Father (Romans 8:15). Only Christians have this relationship, for it is the fruit of being freed from sin and living in Christ.

Secondly, this transforming work of the cross and the Spirit affects the mind of the believer. Instead of our mind being ruled by the passions and desires of our fallen nature as exemplified in what Paul calls the works of the flesh (see Galatians 5:19), we are able to lay aside our "former way of life and the old self which deteriorates through illusion and desire and acquire a fresh, spiritual way of thinking." We can once again become new men and women created in God's image as he had originaly intended (Ephesians 4:22-24; 2 Corinthians 5:17-22). This is a truth little recognized in contemporary spirituality.

The cross of Jesus puts to death our old sinful ways of thinking: lust, greed, resentment and arrogance. We are able to take every thought "into captivity and make it obedient to Christ" (2 Corinthians 10:5). We can have a true renewal of our mind so that we can judge "what is good and pleasing and perfect" (Romans 12:2). This renewal of the mind is the desired end of our spiritual life, for out of our hearts and minds come forth the good deeds done out of love for God and neighbor.

Daily prayer and spiritual exercises need to be centered on the renewal of our minds. This is done through daily examination of conscience and repentance by which the power of sin is conquered; and through daily prayer (private and common) and scripture reading by which the realities of the Gospel become actualities that affect the way we live, think and act. Only in prayer and scripture can the Spirit reveal to us spiritual realities whose grandeur and majesty outshine the fantasies and illusions of sin.

The sacrament of Penance is instrumental in achieving this renewal of the mind. Through confession of sin and the action of Christ himself in the person of the priest, not only is sin forgiven and guilt removed, but the powerful grasp that sin has upon our minds is broken. Our wills are strengthened. This is not a human psychological exercise; it is the power of the cross and resurrection to change our lives through the sacramental action of the Lord Jesus.

A Spirituality of Conversion

By way of conclusion, I would like to make one practical point. The Church today desperately needs a renewal in its spiritual and sacramental life at all levels: among bishops, priests, religious and laity. The Church today is filled with unevangelized, unconverted and uncatechised "Christians." What is needed is not some esoteric spirituality whether it be called creation spirituality or even Franciscan, Ignatian or mystical. On the practical level these "spiritual" cliches often cloud and fudge the real issue which is that people need to hear and submit to the basic Gospel. Often I have preached the basic truths of the Gospel as presented in this paper, and people have said to me: "I am not into that kind of spirituality. I am not into sin, repentance and the cross. I'm into Carmelite mysticism, or creation spirituality or centering prayer." Such comments are a spiritual evasion which prevents the real and true Gospel from penetrating their lives. The recognition of our fallen nature and the conviction of sin has nothing to do with what might be popularly called "Ignatian spirituality," although Ignatius preached it. However, it has everything to do with conversion to the Gospel, as Ignatius knew very well. The power of the cross of Jesus has in a sense nothing to do with Franciscanism, although it was the centerpiece of Francis' preaching, not because it was Francis' "thing," but because it is the heart of the Gospel. Francis was also aware of this. What the people of God need to hear is the Gospel, and if a label must be given, what they need to hear is a spirituality of conversion.

Christians and Catholics need to hear, Sunday after Sunday, that they are fallen human beings and daily sinners. They need to learn and daily practice repentance. They must come to know the power of the cross to change their lives. They must come to appreciate the new life of the resurrection and the Spirit of Jesus. They need to be taught and to practice the life of prayer and scripture reading. This is not a spirituality. This is the simple, but true, life of the Gospel.

If I were to categorize the present spiritual state of the Church, I would say that in many ways we are in a catechumenate state, to use a patristic designation. Many, if not most, of our members have not experienced full conversion. (Pope Paul VI has called attention to this fact in his apostolic Exhortation, *Evangelii Nuntiandi*).

An example that illustrates this catechumenate state is that practicing Catholics and Catholic families go to weekly Sunday Mass and receive communion and yet a substantial majority of these people rarely, if ever, receive the Sacrament of Reconciliation. This is due not to their sinfulness, but rather to their disregard for sin (and even serious sin) and their lack of reverence for the Body and Blood of Christ. We need to take seriously Paul's condemnation of profaning the Eucharist and the resulting judgment that flows from this (see 1 Corinthians 11:27-32).

Because of this present situation, I believe that an emphasis must be placed on evangelizing, catechising and teaching both within and apart from sacramental and liturgical settings. Prior to Vatican II the sacramental action was emphasized in contrast to the Protestant primacy of the word. The Council has restored the Word of God to its proper role within the liturgy and the sacraments. This is admirably appropriate at this time, for only if our people first come to true conversion through the preaching of Gospel and through catechesis will they be able to participate fully in and reap the benefits of the sacraments. As the Fathers of the Church knew well, until someone comes to conversion they cannot truly enter into the full mysteries of the faith - that is the Eucharist. Because of this catechumenate state within the Church, I would propose that our homilies, teaching and instruction follow the *Catechetical Lectures* which St. Cyril of Jerusalem preached to those coming into the Church, rather than his *Mystagogic Lectures* preached to those already converted. Until our Catholic people come to a mature commitment to Jesus in their daily prayer and until the foundational truths of the Gospel become realities in their lives, the full grace of the sacraments, especially Confession and the Eucharist will be of little lasting benefit.

Some of you may question what I have just said, but I speak from experience. I have helped to bring hundreds of people to conversion, both non-believers and so-called practicing Catholics. I do not brag --it is the work of God's mercy and grace -- but I do know that until people are truly converted they cannot reap the marvelous benefits of the sacraments.

It is only when we are daily repenting of our sins, praying, and reading God's word that we are prepared to participate fully in the sacramental mysteries of Christ. Such participation will, in turn, nourish us to love God and to love our neighor here in this life and forever in heaven.

Response to Fr. Weinandy's Paper
by
Mother Assumption Long, O.P.

Father Weinandy has called our attention to the Fall, "the original sin of Adam and Eve by which they lost the divine friendship and preternatural gifts for themselves and all their human progeny" (John A. Hardon, S.J. *Modern Catholic Dictionary*, Doubleday, 1980, p. 206). He has also emphasized the salvific work of Christ as the cornerstone of our Christian spirituality and our sacramental life. It is not possible to speak of any one of these -- Fall, Incarnation, Death, Resurrection, Sacraments, Spirituality -- in an absolutely discrete sense. Each one involves the others from *our* point of view, the point of view of those who come in the historical time after the events of the Fall, Incarnation, Death and Resurrection. Yet it is important to try to separate each one out. It may be partly due to a failure to try to give our attention to each that so-called spirituality today tends to be "resurrectionist" or now "creationist" and so partial and even falsifying.

I. The Fall

The Fall took place. Our race has fallen. *We* have fallen. We have been saved from the Fall by the passion and death of Christ, which expiated human sin and regained what Adam had lost. Sanctifying grace is restored at justification, but the preternatural gifts -- infused knowledge, absence of concupiscence, bodily immortality -- are not ours. The *ability* to overcome concupiscence has been returned, but only as that: the *capacity* to overcome. Bodily immortality has been returned, but only *eventually*, after the final resurrection (*Ibid.*, p. 395).

There is no doubt that many today think of themselves as good Catholics because of their affection or sentiment for belonging to the church and their false ideas about the right to differ with (dissent from) the teachings of the Church. These Catholics speak as if knowledge is infused and the overcoming of concupiscense is a pre-Vatican II preoccupation of the scrupulous. Father Weinandy has delineated this problem in his discussion of "spiritual evasionism" which, of course, is connected with "spiritual consumerism." If "centering prayer" is in vogue, that can be the excuse not to pay attention to eradicating sin. If "creation spirituality" is the latest fad, then that can be the distraction, the evasion, of something more fundamental. Religious people -- priests, sisters, lay people -- in the middle of ordinary conversation announce that someone is "anti-incarnational." All of this indicates a certain lack of seriousness.

II. The Incarnation

"The Son of God assumed our flesh, body and soul, and dwelled among us, like one of us, in order to redeem us" (Hardon, p. 272). Jesus' conduct is shown in the New Testament as a ministering and self-surrendering love, a love for us, a love that gets involved with us. We accept this love. It is communicated to us. We imitate it and hand it on. (cf. Ratzinger, Schurmann, and Von Balthaser, *Principles of Christian Morality,* Ignatius Press, 1986, p. 20). Thus it is a grave error to suppose that we do not have to strive to conduct ourselves as Jesus conducted Himself.

III. Death

Christ died for our sins. "If we say that we have not sinned, we make God a liar" (1 John 1:10). We have moral guilt; this guilt is sin. Such guilt and sin must be referred to Christ. We are responsible before Him. He bore our guilt on the Cross. Our sin is not *mere* guilt, something to be purged through psychology or sociology (cf. Ratzinger, et al, pp. 87-88). The Cross is the cause of redemption from sin (cf. Hardon, p. 466).

IV. Resurrection

But Christ has risen and thus victoriously completed the redemption of man from sin and death. By his Cross and Resurrection we have been set free from sin (*Ibid*).

V. Sacraments and Spiritual Life

The fullness of grace was made available through the visible channels merited and established by Christ (*Ibid.*, p. 477). There is truly no spiritual life for us, as Father Weinandy has seen with such Catholic insight, without the sacraments. They are the beginning, the progress, and the consummation of our spiritual life. We must live from Mass to Mass; from Holy Communion to Holy Communion; from Adoration of the Blessed Sacrament to Adoration of the Blessed Sacrament; from Visit to Visit to Christ in the Eucharist; from meditation to meditation; from cleansing and healing to cleansing and healing in the Sacrament of Penance. Our daily lives have to be marked by these sacramental encounters. All that intervenes -- whatever our work may be -- must be preparation for and fruit of this sacramental life. If such is our life, it will be a life that follows and imitates Christ's life. In his death is our death to our merely human self; in his rising is our rising from selfishness, pride and sensuality to generosity and self-discipline and the love of charity.

This is no call sadness but rather to gladness. Gladness is the result of interior happiness. It is shown externally -- even if facial expression. Cheerfulness is the emotional side of spiritual well-being. (*Ibid.*, p. 231). Since the sacraments confer grace, and sanctifying grace is an infusion by God, and this grace belongs to the mind, will and affections (*Ibid.*, p. 488), it can only have the effect of joy and gladness. But the basis of this human flourishing or well-being is spiritual, interior.

Father Weinandy alluded in different ways to our need for Penance, both as a sacrament and as a practice. We are, indeed, catechumens, who are not fully converted. Father said: "The Church today is filled with unevangelized, unconverted and uncatechised 'Christians.' " This is a startling statement, yet somehow many, many minds *have* taken on a purely naturalistic caste. The actions -- and the talk -- are all too human. One hears cries for "positive thinking," abhorrence of penance in any form, no love of the Cross. We are *not* O.K.

The great saints did not say so. In an article that appeared in the Fall, 1985 issue of *Communio*, Father Chantraine speaks of a "scraping away" of the self that is necessary for true prayer. He says that "this scouring does not take on its ecclesial dimension except in the sacrament of Penance." (Georges Chantraine, "Prayer Within the Church," *Communio*, Fall, 1985, p. 262).

The truth that the sacraments are each specific ways to be united to Christ is an important one, and one that is often blurred today. The July 1986 *Homiletic and Pastoral Review* contains a brave article by Christopher Derrick entitled "On *Not* Receiving the Lord." I take it that Mr. Derrick is arguing for some way out of what he sees as a situation that does not seem to make provision for the human condition, as realistically considered. The removal of the requirement of the fast before reception of the Holy Communion *does* leave those who refrain in an awkward position. Of drastically greater importance, Mr. Derrick sees this situation as one that can lead to sacriligious Communion. What should be noticed here is the real concern that the Sacrament be reverenced, that it be *believed* to be a specific union with Christ, distinguished from any other sacrament or any other action.

VI. The Cross

It might be that we are afflicted in the Church today with a lack of realism, in several senses of this word. For isn't the erroneous equation between happiness and lack of suffering a lack of spiritual realism? Aren't we affected by the hedonistic, emotivist, and utilitarian philosophies of the world? For the natural man, the greatest mystery of the saints is this: "the more they suffer, the more perfect is their happiness, their peace, their joy." (Jan-Hendirk Walgrave, O.P., "Prayer and Mysticism," *Communio*, Fall, 1985, p. 289). Thus Father Weinandy holds up for our contemplation the Cross on which "Christ has died." Christ is risen and Christ will come again. Cardinal Ratzinger has written that the reflections and questionings of the scholars are "nothing but idle verbiage unless... backed up by a

Christian existence that has learned to discern the spirits in the 'Passion' of everday life." (Ratzinger *et al.*, p. 73).

Spirituality and the Religious Life
by
Fr. Jonathan Robinson

This paper has two related themes. The first of these concerns the ways in which interpretations of the decree *Perfectae Caritatis* (Concerning Religious Life)[1] have deflected the proper implementation of the decree. These interpretations have opened the way to the seepage of error and bad practice into the theory and practice of spirituality. The second theme deals with some of the basic elements of Catholic spirituality which need to be re-emphasized today.

These two themes complement each other. The abstract and unrealistic character of many of the interpretations of *Perfectae Caritatis* points to a need for a more concrete or practical foundation for religious life. This concrete or practical foundation is to be found, I maintain, in the traditional spirituality of the Church. It is precisely in those ascetical and moralistic elements of the spiritual life which are so often in practice ignored and even openly derided that we will find, once again, the foundation for a happy and a fruitful religious life.

I want to add, at the end of my paper, that the blame for the present situation is, in part, to be laid at the door of those who supported and taught the traditional spirituality of the Church. Either they misunderstood their own tradition, or else they were frightened of it. In either case we have paid dearly for ignorance or timidity.

I

Both the Document on the Church[2] and the Document on Religious emphasize that everyone is called to holiness. In itself, this is hardly a new idea. St. Philip Neri said: "Let persons in the world sanctify themselves in their own houses, for neither the court, professions, or labour are any hindrance to the service of God."[3] St. Francis de Sales and St. Ignatius aimed at teaching holiness to those living both outside and inside formal religious structures.

So far as I can understand it, the Fathers of the Council wanted to emphasize that the fullness of the Christian life was possible outside an enclosed monastery. Christian perfection, or holiness, or whatever we are going to call it, cannot be identified with the contemplative vocation understood as an institutionalized form of this life. On the other hand, we should note carefully that the Council does not say that the perfection of the Christian life cannot be found in a contemplative monastery. In fact, it says just the reverse:

> Members of those communities which are totally dedicated to contemplation give themselves to God alone in solitude and silence and through constant prayer and ready penance. No

matter how urgent may be the needs of the active apostolate, such communities will always have a distinguished part to play in Christ's Mystical Body...[4]

This passage shows you cannot argue that the Council taught that only a life of prayer which issues in an active apostolate is authentically Catholic. Holiness is open to all - even to contemplatives!

This relatively straightforward position has become entangled at the theological level with a number of other questions. The theologians wanted a re-examination of the relation between the commandments and the counsels. In particular, they were keen on a revision of St. Thomas' teaching on the relation of the counsels to the religious life, and of the commandments to secular life. This question then involved a consideration of the nature of the element of law in the Christian life. This consideration (on the role of law) was, in its turn, enmeshed in lucubrations of uncertain import on following and imitating Christ.

The document itself very prudently leaves a great deal undecided. You can read about the various forces and compromises which went into the finished product by consulting Volume 2 of Herbert Vorgrimier's *Commentary on the Documents of Vatican II*. Friedrich Wulf, the Editor of the Commentary on *Perfectae Caritatis*,[5] also wrote the Introduction and the Commentary on Chapter 5 and 6 of the Constitution on the Church. In reference to Chapter 5 of this Constitution, he writes:

Casting an eye... over Chapter 5, we are forced to say that hardly an ecclesiastical document of recent times could be found which so often and so forcefully proclaims the grace-given, charismatic nature of Christian life - of sanctification and the pursuit of perfection. This seems to dispose at last of the ascetical approach that has dominated Catholic piety for so long, especially since the nineteenth century.[6]

The thinking represented in this passage seems to me to be the *fons et origo* of many contemporary difficulties in religious life today. It is a type of thinking which argues for many true and important propositions. Yet, these very truths have been taken out of their proper context, and they have been applied in a way that has harmed rather than aided the flourishing of religious life.

In trying to explain my meaning, I want to make three points.

The first of these concerns the use of history. Catholicism is a historical religion. It makes certain claims about events which happened in the past. The understanding of these events, and, in a way, the reality of the events, is committed to the Church. It is the Church which carries the understanding and the reality of these events through time. It follows from this that the authentic witnesses to this tradition have to be studied and understood if we are to understand what Christianity means.

When it comes to the question of religious life, we have to study and understand not only the Bible and the work of the theologians, but also how the great founders and reformers of religious orders understood religious life. We must do this because they are the authentic witnesses to that part of revelation which pertains to living a holy life at the end of the 16th century, Fr. Consolini, St. Philip's confidant during the last years of the Saint's life, wrote on a draft of the Constitutions of the Oratory the words of Isaiah: "Look to the rock from which you were hewn, and the pit from which you were dug."[7] Fr. Consolini's action represents the proper spirit. By all means read your Freud and Weber, but certainly not to find out how to live the religious life.

This appeal to the authority of the founders and reformers is urged by the Decree on Religious: "...loyal recognition and safekeeping should be accorded to the spirit of founders, as also to all the particular goals and wholesome traditions which constitute the heritage of each community."[8]

This injunction, an injunction which is essential to an understanding of religious life, has been wrongly used. In many religious orders, the only aspects of the Founder's intentions and spirit which are retained serve as a basis for a propositional function. The propositional function goes something like this: "Founder X always has a relation to time Y. The only thing we are bound by is the formal relationship between X and Y." Using this empty proposition as a first principle, the argument then goes on as follows: "We are not X, and we do not live in time Y. Therefore, nothing that was actually said or done in the past has any interest, other than nostalgic or antiquarian. It is certainly not binding in the here and now."

My second point concerns the question of following and imitating Christ.[9] Catholicism has always maintained that following Christ involves a call to imitate him. Augustine said: "Quid enim sequi nisi imitari?"[10] That is, what does follow mean except to imitate? For Augustine following means imitating, and the spirituality of the Christian was seen as an effort to become like Christ. In *Philippians*, St. paul says: "Him I would learn to know, and the virtue of his resurrection, and what it means to share his sufferings, moulded (*morphizomenos - configuratus*) into the pattern of his death, in the hope of achieving resurrection from the dead."[11] This moulding, this configuring, into the pattern of Christ's death is God's work as well as ours. It is what Catholics have understood by the imitation of Christ.

Luther saw in this call to imitate Christ just one more pride-filled and futile effort of sinful man to acquire merit. Faith, for Luther, meant following Christ in obedience, and it was this faith which justified man before God. Practising the virtues does not, he thought, have any significance for justification. According to Luther, we follow in faith, and Christ's merits cover us; but our sinful nature remains unchanged.[12] In itself, such a theory is not incompatible with a moral life, but it easily gives way to the thought that since morality is not necessary for salvation, it is not important.

It may be the case that Catholics used to talk too much about virtues in relation to the spiritual life. Yet, imitating Christ is not like copying a secular hero we have chosen for ourselves, and whom we reproduce in ourselves by our own unaided efforts. Such an attitude is Pelagian rather than Catholic.

Insofar as Catholics had fallen into this way of thinking and acting, some sort of redress was necessary. Nevertheless, it is a gross error to conclude that the way we redress the balance is to forget altogether about the need to fight against sin, and the obligation to cultivate the virtues. The first stage of the spiritual life, according to St. Thomas, is concerned with pulling up the roots of our attraction to sin.[13] A great deal of what we hear in the Church today concerning spirituality seems to imagine that there are no longer any beginners, and that purgation of sin is no longer an important element in the life of a mature Christian. This is wicked and pernicious nonsense.

Behind this nonsense is a new development in moral theology which demands our attention. Consider the following lines from Friedrich Wulf:

> Anyone who lives by this imparting of grace knows ultimately how to fulfill but one commandment in all the separate precepts: the commandment to love. This cannot be restricted to specific, fixed, precisely recognizable duties, but is in fact without any limits. In all his objective and universal obligation to the moral demands of the second table of the decalogue, in all the exigencies and situations of his life, he knows that he lives under the ever present, personal call of God, a call that lures and leads to love. How this imperative is best applied to the here and now of each passing hour cannot be deduced solely from rational considerations however Christian.[14]

No one can doubt that these lines are very moving. The question is, what do they mean, and how are they liable to be interpreted? Well, we all know at least how this sort of writing has been interpreted. Imitating Christ, living without regard for the law as law, had led to the same doctrine as that held by the radical Franciscans in the 14th century. There are lots of names for this perversion of Christianity. Antinomianism, I suppose, is the classic term. Jacopone da Todi, in one of his *Lauds* describes it this way:

> For this love without faith,
> (Love gone astray), there is no sin.

> This is abominable teaching, heresy!
> All men do well to avoid its company.[15]

I am not saying, of course, that all followers of the new trends in moral theology are antinomians. I am saying, however, that their teaching has been interpreted in a way which often seems to make the practical consequences of their teaching indistinguishable from that castigated by Jacopone, I think that it is significant that in the traditional account of the development of the spiritual life, the imitation of Christ was placed in the illuminative way, the way of the proficients to use St. Thomas' vocabulary.[16] In other words, it was time to talk about being led by the spirit and interpreting the demands of the Christian life in terms of love when the elements of morality had been achieved. In the case of religious, it seems to me, we would have to add that they are led by the spirit and not by law, if and when the elements of poverty, chastity and obedience have been acquired.

Aristotle says only someone who has been well brought up can hope to live a good life.[17] If a religious has not been taught to practice obedience, to value his chastity, and to practice poverty, as his Institute understands it, how can he hope to live as God wants him to?

Certainly, the first inclination to quit undertakings solemnly and freely undertaken should not be looked on as an expression of a "grace-given, charismatic expression of the Christian life." The desire to live high, to be unchaste, and to refuse to do what we are told, are just what they used to be, that is temptations. If we yield to temptation, it is sin.

This leads to the third consideration.

There is great stress in much of the writing about the Council documents on the fact that it is the Church which is indefectibly holy, and that "the holiness of the individual is always a mere participation in the holiness of the Church, proclaiming to the world, as it must, the holiness of the Church."[18]

> ...so far as the constitution is concerned, Christian holiness is not primarily - much less exclusively - moral perfection, heroic human virtue, but primarily and in the deepest sense the glory and the love of God given to the redeemed without any merit on their part...
> ...those whom God calls to holiness do not receive the holiness of Christ directly, in a purely private personal encounter between two persons, but in the Church (the community of the People of God) and by her intermediary. (sic)[19]

Now this is all splendid and inspiring, but it has been badly used. Even if we do not receive the holiness of Christ directly but only through the Church and its sacraments, nevertheless, it is individuals who receive it. I think we have been hypnotized, bamboozled into a way of thinking which is almost indistinguishable from the most exteme *ex opere operato* thinking which the Council set out to correct. That is, because the Church is holy, and because the counsels belong to the Church, then it hardly matters what we do, so long as we have been baptized into the People of God, and, of course, keep our fundamental option open.

It is almost as though something like the following is being said. "Given the holiness of Christ and of his Church, it would betray the mentality of a bookkeeper to worry too much about how *I* behave. The new Biblical exegesis has revealed to us the great, splendid, wide open spaces where the wind of the Spirit of God blows freely where it will - do we want to try to contain this Spirit within the narrow, petty, and inward looking confines of the moral view of life? Surely mature and responsible Christians have too broad a view of things to concern themselves with the personal striving and the personal failures of people obsessed with an individualistic and law-oriented morality. Perhaps it even show a lack of trusting faith to be concerned with what *I* do or don't do."

This sort of thinking is lethal and is all around us. Without our efforts to live the moral law, to draw away from sin, and to practice the virtues, we are in the gravest danger of becoming self-serving hypocrites, who, at best, use the Christian vocabulary to cover our own lack of generosity and self-sacrifice, and, at worst, use the religious profession to cover an immoral life-style.[20] Let me cite the following words of a modern Carmelite, Ruth Burrows:

> Let us remind ourselves over and over again that holiness has to do with very ordinary things: truthfulness, courtesy, kindness, gentleness, consideration for others, contentment with our lot, honesty and courage in the face of life, reliability, dutifulness. Intent, as we think, on the higher reaches of spirituality, we can overlook the warp and woof of holiness.[21]

In sum, then, a belief in the holiness of the Church is no substitute for the efforts of individuals to strive after holiness themselves. This striving after holiness means following Christ in an effort to imitate him. We cannot imitate Christ unless we make war on the law of sin in ourselves and strive to obey the moral law. Finally, the way in which we discover how the moral life applies to a particular form of the religious life is by a serious, sustained and reverent effort to understand the historical givenness of the founder's understanding of his vocation.

II

Having shown how history, morality and holiness have been badly understood in the Post-Conciliar years, I want now to indicate how the remedy is to be found in the traditional spirituality of the Church.

According to the teaching of St. Augustine and St. Thomas, there is an ordered progress of development in the growth of charity in the life of a Christian. There are three main stages in this development which are those of the beginner, of the proficient, and of the perfect. It has to be admitted that the words do not ring happily in modern ears. I think, however, that the tradition is talking about something that has not changed and we must make do with the vocabulary until something better is found.

A more serious difficulty concerns there being stages in what is, after all, a living process of growth. I think it is important to notice that Thomas does not call them stages but *studia*.[22] The word *studium* indicates whatever is of overwhelming interest, or the primary focus of attention, for a person. I do not see that Thomas' position involves holding that I am successful or otherwise in what it is that rivets my attention. What Thomas is saying is that at different periods in our lives there are certain dominant themes or interests. He is not saying that the concerns of the other stages disappear with a shift in preoccupation. He writes as follows:

> ...the different stages of charity can be marked according as growth in charity leads a man to fix his main attention on different things. For, to begin with, he must devote himself mainly to withdrawing from sin and resisting the appetites, which drive him in the opposite direction to charity. This is the condition of beginners, who need to nourish and carefully foster charity to prevent its being lost.[23]

I think that a great deal of writing about spirituality today ignores this first *studium* of St. Thomas. St. Thomas says that at the beginning we must concentrate on withdrawing from sin and on resisting the appetites which drive us in the opposite direction to charity. Those words are as true today as they were when he wrote them.

A great writer on prayer, Abbot Chapman of Downside,[24] said that good people distrust mysticism for the same reason that bad people like it. Those words were written in the early thirties, and they are even more apt today. There are any number of books and approaches to prayer which seem to concentrate on the techniques of prayer divorced from any theological or moral context. It is almost as though the opinion makers having recommended drink, sex and drugs, now teach that meditation has become the latest trip. God can bring good out of anything he chooses, but, on the face of it, a life formed by the counter-culture, as it was called ten years ago, is not the best foundation for the spiritual life.

In connection with the first *studium*, there are three things I want to talk about: Jesus Christ, meditation, and the link between mortification and self-knowledge.

1. Jesus Christ

St. John tells us in his Gospel that "no one has ever seen God" and then goes on to say that "the only Son, who is in the bosom of the Father, he has made him known."[25] If we know what God is like only through the Son, then we have no standard, neither intellectual nor moral nor empirical, by which we could forsee or determine the nature of God's self-giving. This entails that we will have to take seriously the fact of the revealing of the unknown God. The operative word here is *accept*. God reveals, and we accept or reject. If we accept God's revelation as contained in the preaching and tradition of the Church, we must take seriously our Lord's words that he is the way, the truth, and the life and take to heart his teaching that no one goes to the Father except through Him.

I am perfectly aware that what I have just said is rejected by many people today. Revelation, we are told on all sides, is not propositional. The contention seems to be that while revelation informs us about matters which are frightfully important, it doesn't inform us about anything in particular. St. Thomas teaches that the object of faith is the First Truth[26] (which is simple),[27] nonetheless, this truth is received by us in the form of propositions (*enuntiabilia*). These *enuntiabilia* are the material object of faith.[28] Faith is about statements the human mind can understand, and then either reject or accept. Of course there is a great deal more to the object of faith than what can be understood; nor have I said anything about faith as a virtue. Yet it does not follow from this that the mind has no role in our life of faith.

Catholicism is a religion which claims to be true. Right thinking about faith, orthodoxy as the assent to the truths of our faith, is an essential aspect of our life of prayer. Prayer without true belief lacks intellectual structure and moral content. Prayer such as this quickly degenerates into a sentimental expression of a sense of unity with either God or the group or both. If it does not degenerate in this way, then it quickly begins to become a pointless exercise, an exercise irrelevant to the pressing demands of daily life.

As Catholics, we have to begin with Jesus Christ and what he taught us. Our appropriation through prayer of the truths of our faith must begin (and end) with what we believe to be true about him.

2. Meditation.

Christian meditation means trying to assimilate God's revelation to us in Christ and to do this in a way that touches us personally.

God respects what he had created, and prayer must begin by the use of the ordinary faculties he has given us - the understanding, will, imagination and memory. St. John of the Cross says:

> ...meditation is a discursive action wrought by means of images, forms and figures that are fashioned and imagined by the senses, as when we imagine Christ crucified, or bound to a column, or at another of the stations... or when we imagine all kinds of other

things, whether Divine or human, that can belong to the imagination ...these meditations are necessary to beginners, in order that they may gradually feed and enkindle their souls with love by means of sense.[29]

Today there are many people who teach what they call meditation, but it does not meet the definition of St. John of the Cross. For these people, meditation seems to consist in an effort to hypnotize or, at least, still the will, the memory, the understanding, and the imagination in order to achieve a state of quietude which they mistake for contemplation.

The writer of *The Cloud of Unknowing*, one of the most severely mystical books on prayer ever written, is insistent that it is only through meditating that we begin our life of prayer. Thus he writes:

...whosoever man or woman weeneth to come to contemplation without many such sweet meditations beforehand of his own wretchedness, the passion, the kindness, the great goodness, and the worthiness of God, surely he shall err and fail of his purpose... the lower part of the contemplative life lieth in good ghostly meditations, and busy beholding unto man's own wretchedness with sorrow and contrition, unto the passion of Christ and of his servants with pity and compassion, and unto the wonderful gifts, kindness, and works of God in all his creatures, bodily and ghostly, with thanking and praising.[30]

St. Teresa says "God gave us our faculties to work with, and everything will have its due reward; there is no reason, then, for trying to cast a spell over them - they must be allowed to perform their office until God gives them a better one."[31]

It is clear from this testimony that meditation is an essential step to a closer union with God in prayer. I would like to go into St. Teresa's teaching as to why we must begin with meditation, but perhaps you will think I am labouring the point to no purpose. There is, however, a purpose, and it is a purpose which touches contemporary concerns.

The effort to bypass meditation represents an effort to achieve a state of contemplation in which the awareness of God's activity is increasingly apparent without waiting for the proper signs[32] and without the proper preparation. At best, the effort to skip meditation seems to be a mistake. For, as St. John of the Cross says, if we turn aside from meditation too soon, the soul will have no occupation, "but will be wholly idle, and there would be no way in which it could be said to be employed."[33]

It is said the devil finds work for idle hands. Certainly he finds work for idle minds. The purpose of our prayer in the first *Studium* is to help us to withdraw from sin and resist the appetites. That requires we use our heads to see our own lives in relation to the law of God, and our wills to try to keep this law. To induce a state of quietude by natural techniques is perfectly compatible with living an immoral life, and even with refusing to admit the existence of Christian norms.

If the way to the Father is through the Son, we have to learn about the Son in a way that affects our own lives. St. Francis de Sales says that we "think of divine things not to learn, but to make ourselves love them."[34] We meditate in order to move the affections. St. Paul says: "Think diligently upon him that endured such opposition from sinners against himself; that you be not wearied, fainting in your minds."[35] St. Francis de Sales comments on this text in the following way:

> When (St. Paul) says think diligently upon him that endured such opposition from sinners against himself that you be not wearied, fainting in your minds, it is as though he said meditate. But why would he have us to meditate on the holy passion? Not that we should become learned, but what we should become patient and constant in the ways of heaven. O how I have loved thy law O Lord, says David: It is my meditation all the day. He meditates on the law because he loves it and he loves it because he meditates on it.[36]

3. Self-Knowledge and Mortification.

The Oracle at Delphi said "Know Thyself." Today there is a lot of concern for self-awareness, and we are said to be living in a subjective age, an age, that is, which is concerned with the individual and his feelings, ambitions, and character. It is an age which prides itself on self-knowledge and authenticity.

Very often the way this self-knowledge is supposed to be achieved is through introspection. We are told to look inside ourselves and see how we are feeling and reacting to the different situations of life. This can become a misleading and a dangerous activity. It becomes misleading when we think we are discovering our real self, holding it up like an object for our own inspection. Obviously we are not seeing all of ourselves, for who or what is doing the looking? What we are really doing is observing one aspect of ourselves and, without some control, we select what suits us. Very quickly we build up an image of ourselves which is, at best, selective, and, at worst, false and misleading. This becomes dangerous when we take, as we nearly always do, this constructed and selective self to be the real self. This is a very common procedure and explains why so often people seem to have absolutely no capacity to understand their behaviour and how their behaviour affect other people. It is also the reason the tradition insisted on a regular confessor.

The whole topic of self-deception has received a great deal of scrutiny in modern British and American philosophy.[37] It seems to me extraordinary that this theme, which is one found in so many masters of the spiritual life, should be so ignored -- and ignored precisely by those who pride themselves on their intimate relationship with the signs of the times. Left to ourselves we fool ourselves, and nowhere is this more true than in the effort to love and to serve God.

How is self-knowledge to be acquired? It is acquired by cooperating with the pattern of suffering and of healing, of dying and of resurrection, which we find in the Bible and enshrined in all Catholic spirituality. In the Book of Deuteronomy we find the following passage:

> See now that I, even I, am he,
> and there is no God besides me;
> I kill and I make alive;
> I wound and I heal; and there is
> none that can deliver out of my hand.[38]

This work of God, this wounding in order to heal, of killing in order to bring to life again, is found all through the Old and the New Testaments and reaches its summit in Christ.

In Christian thought, the effort to cooperate with the pattern of suffering and of healing, of dying and of resurrection, is called *mortification*.[39] The writer of *The Imitation of Christ* writes as follows about the need for a voluntary acceptance of suffering:

> Behold, then, how in the cross all things stand; and how, in dying to the world, lies all our health; and that there is no other way to life and true inward peace but the way of the cross, and the way of daily submission of the body to the spirit. Go wherever you will, and reap whatever you desire, and you will never find above you or beneath you, within you or without you, a more high, a more excellent, a more sure way to Christ than the way of the Holy Cross.[40]

One of the fruits of mortification is self-knowledge. When we try to say no to the things that please us and when we are forced to face up to real internal and external difficulties, we very quickly discover of what stuff we are made. We find it is difficult to say no to pleasure and satisfactions of various sorts; and we also find the limits of our courage, our endurance and our generosity. The self-knowledge that comes from these experiences is not flattering. On the other hand, it is usually true. Being true, it shows us what we really are, and how far we have still to go.

What we are forced to recognize is the truth that we are wounded by original sin, that we ourselves sin, that we are weak, and that we need God. All these unpleasant and unsatisfactory truths have to be acknowledged by us in a real and effective way if we are ever going to find, to recognize, and to accept what God wants to give us.

> Behold, thou desirest truth in my inward being;
> therefore teach me wisdom in my secret heart.[41]

The Second Studium.

St. John of the Cross and others associate this *studium* with the beginning of contemplation which appears, from one point fo view, as

God taking an active part in our efforts to mortify ourselves. I am sure that much of the legitimate dissatisfaction with the way spirituality was sometimes presented in the past is that contemplation and the beginnings of the illuminative way were looked on as being of very rare occurrence and even as being somehow reprehensible. St. John of the Cross has some harsh things to say about directors who do not or cannot recognize the signs that God is beginning to lead the penitent in a new way and who attempt to force the penitent back into the first *studium*.[42]

The doctrine of St. John of the Cross did not originate with him. It is found, to name but a few, in St. Gregory the Great, in Hugh of St. Victor and in Tauler. All these teachers emphasize the positive aspect of the matter: the burning desire for God and for perfection. They all view the *studium* as a sign of great progress and the result of a deep working of grace. It is the divine action on us which is the principal element in the matter. This action of God on us manifests itself in the first place as dryness and the practical impossibility to meditate.

Abbot Chapman describes it this way:

> .... a penitent comes and says he cannot meditate; that all feelings of love have gone; that he can't examine his conscience though something automatic happens instead; that he can't make good resolutions, only somehow he wants to keep close to God (only that seems to mean nothing in particular); and that he is quite sure he has no virtues, and never practices any; and his prayer is only distraction. Only he has no sins to confess except what the confessor cannot accept as matter.[43]

This condition among good people who try to pray is not uncommon. It has to be recognized that a new element has entered into the situation. God is taking a more obvious and direct action in the life of the penitent. The Gift of Wisdom has begun its work, and a new start has to be made. It is the beginning of the illuminative way, a way in which the soul is taught and led by God in a manner it often does not understand.

St. John of the Cross says that the purpose of walking is to arrive and not to walk. The purpose of meditation and good resolutions, of active mortification and especially of obedience, is to prepare us for God's action, an action which, if we are faithful, will lead to the union of our will with the will of our Creator - but that is another and even longer story. It is, however, a story that gives meaning, rest and hope to those who seek to respond to Christ's invitation: "Rise up and follow me." If it was not widely taught in the past, then it is hardly surprising so much of the house has come tumbling down.

On the other hand, it is a story we will never even begin to understand if we try to take short cuts.

1. Decree on the Appropriate Renewal of the Religious Life. *Perfectae Caritatis.*

2. Dogmatic Constitution on the Church, *Lumen Gentium.*

3. *Maxims and Counsels of St. Philip Neri, Arranged for Every Day in the Year.* Dublin 1890. Maxim for Jan. 20.

4. *Perfectae Caritatis*, Sec. 7.

5. *Commentary of the Documents of Vatican II*, ed. Herbert Vorgrimler, Herder and Herder, Vol. 2, pp 301-370.

6. *Ibid.* p. 272.

7. *Isaiah.* 51:1.

8. *Perfectae Caritatis*, Sec. 2b.

9. See the article "Imitation du Christ." *Dictionnaire de Spiritualite*, Tome VII, cols. 1536-1630.

10. *De Sancta Virginitate*, 17.

11. Phil. 3:10-11.

12. "Justification calls for three things, and three things only: God's grace, Christs's merit, and faith. Faith, moreover, takes a hold of the very gifts God promises in the Gospel; and on its account the righteousness of Christ is deemed ours. Through it also we have our sins forgiven; we are reconciled with God; and we become his adopted children and heirs of eternal life." *Solida Declaratio*, cited in *New Catholic Encyclopedia*, art "Lutheranism."

13. *Summa Theologiae*, II, II, 24, 9.

14. *Commentary*, Vol. 2, p. 311.

15. *Laud*, number 33.

16. A Tanquerey, *The Spiritual Life*, Part II, Book II. R. Garrigou-Lagrange, *The Three Ages of the Interior Life*, Part III, Chapter xxvii. *Dictionnaire de Spiritualite* loc. cit.

17. *E.N.* 1095b.

18. *Commentary*, Vol. 1, p. 263.

19. *Ibid.* I suppose the translator means *mediation* and not *intermediary.*

20. It is easy to parody Luther, but even such a learned and sympathetic writer as Fr. Bouyer can write: "(Luther) for want of an adequate expression... pushed to the furthest extreme the one

most inadequate for affirming (his) personalism: namely forensic justification. Going against all ideas of man possessing merits of his own outside the living relationship with Christ, he proclaimed that Christ saves us by faith, but without having to change us in any way, therefore without faith having to be 'informed' (as the Schoolmen said) by love, and he did this precisely so as to maintain that we cannot be saved except in the relationship wherein Christ establishes us with him." *Orthodox Spirituality and Protestant Spirituality*, New York, 1969 p. 67.

My point, of course, is that a great many Catholics today talk as though the popular conception of Luther and his influence were true.

21. Ruth Burrows, *Interior Castle Explored*, London 1981. p. 19.

22. *Summa.* II, II, 24, 9.

23. *Ibid* Prima Pars, 16, 6.

24. *Spiritual Letters*, Reprinted London 1983. "Bad people love bad mysticism, because they think it is occultism or magic. Good people dislike it for almost the same reason." p. 269.

25. John 1:18.

26. *Summa*, II, II, 1, 1.

27. *Ibid*. Prima Pars, 16, 6.

28. *Ibid*, II, II, 1, 2.

29. *Ascent of Mount Carmel*, Book 2, Ch. 12, sec. 5. "St. John also knows a higher form of meditation. Here the imagination looks upon the events described in the Gospel, seeks to exhaust all their meaning and considers with the understanding their general significance and the demands they make. The will is thereby inclined to love, resolving henceforth to live in the spirit of faith." Edith Stein, *The Doctrine of the Cross*, London 1960, p. 85.

30. Chapter 7.

31. *Interior Castle*, IV, iii.

32. St. John of the Cross discusses these signs in the *Ascent of Mount Carmel*, II, 13; and in the *Dark Night of the Soul*, I:9.

33. *Ascent of Mount Carmel*, II, 14, 7. St. John teaches that the way to contemplation is through meditation on the mystery of Christ: "...let him have a habitual desire to imitate Christ in everything that he does, conforming himself to His life; upon which life he must meditate so that he may know how to imitate it, and to behave in all

things as Christ would behave." *Ibid,* Prologue. St. Teresa teaches the same lesson: "...we must not presume or think we can suspend (the understanding) ourselves; nor yet must we allow it to cease working: if we do, we shall remain stupid and cold and shall achieve nothing whatsoever". *Life..* Ch. XII.

34. *Treatise on the Love of God,* Book 6, Ch. 2.

35. Hebrews 12:3.

36. *Treatise on the Love of God, loc. cit.*

37. Herbert Fingarette, *Self Deception,* London 1969, has an extensive bibliography. The subject was debated in the *Proceedings of the Aristotelian Society* during the seventies, and there are several excellent longer studies.

38. Deut. 32:39.

39. For an admirable modern discussion of this topic the article "Mortification" in the *Dictionnaire de Spiritualite,* Fascicules lxx-lxxi, cols 1791-1799, should be consulted.

40. Book 2, Chapter 12.

41. Psalm 51.

42. *The Living Flame of Love,* Stanza III pars. 34-35, first redaction, (The material is also to be found in the second redaction). Incompetent spiritual directors are one of "the three blind guides of the soul," the other two being the self and the devil. The Saint is very harsh: "And our Saviour says: 'Woe unto you that have taken away the key of knowledge, and enter not in yourselves nor allow others to enter!' For these persons in truth are placed like barriers and obstacles at the gate of Heaven, remembering not that God has placed them there that they may compel those whom god calls to enter in, as He has commanded; whereas they on the other hand, are compelling souls not to enter in by the narrow gate that leads to life; in this way such a man is a blind guide who can obstruct the guidance of the Holy Spirit in the soul. This comes to pass in many ways, as has here been said; some do it knowingly, others unconsciously; but neither class shall remain unpunished since having assumed their office they are under an obligation to know and consider what they do." par. 53.

43. Chapman. *Op. cit.* p. 320.

Spiritual Direction in the Church
by
John Sheets, S.J.

1. The Nature of Spiritual Direction

Before we talk about spiritual direction in the Church, it is important to clarify what is meant by the term, and to see how spiritual direction in the Church differs from the practice found among all peoples where those who are wiser counsel those seeking direction.

It is simply a matter of fact that among all peoples those who are endowed with greater gifts instruct those who are not. The gifts might come from special gifts of temperament, training, together with widsom and practical judgment gained from long experience. This type of direction takes many forms, teacher-student, religious leader and disciple, parents and children, elders in a community and those who are less experienced. In the religions of India, special importance is given to the guru (literally, "the venerable one") in his role of guiding others to a high level of spiritual development.

When we speak of spiritual direction in the Church, we are talking about something which is radically different. There are some similarities, but spiritual direction takes on an entirely new meaning, when the "old creation" is transformed into what St. Paul calls the "New Creation" (2 *Co.*: 5. 17). Here again the old dictum is verified: "Grace builds on nature." The natural dynamics at work are taken up into a whole new network of relationships.

The simplest way to approach the topic of spiritual direction is to look at the two words: "spiritual " and "direction." To help us understand what is meant by these words, I want to use a term which C.S. Lewis often employs. It is what he calls "transposition." It means tha putting of the higher into the lower. As mysterious as that sounds, it is something that we are doing at practically every moment of our lives. For example, transposition is at work when our ideas (the higher) are put into words, into movements of air, or into little marks on a sheet of paper (the lower). When an artist puts his inspiration into an arrangement of paint on a canvas, he is transposing the higher into the lower. On another level, we speak of the soul transposed into the body. In a most special instance, we speak of the Incarnation, that is, the transposition of the Word who is with the Father into our human flesh.

How does this term, "transposition," help us understand the meaning of "spiritual direction?" The deepest meaning of our Christian lives is the metamorphosis, the complete change of our being, the

New Creation, that comes through the transposition of the Holy Spirit into our human selves. "God's love has flooded our inmost heart through the Holy Spirit he has given us" (*Rm.:* 5.5).

In the Christian sense, then, "spiritual" does not mean ghostly. Nor does it primarily mean what is immaterial or what cannot be seen. Rather it means that our human spirit, our whole self, has been overshadowed by the Spirit to bring about a New Creation. It is a change of identity. As Paul puts it: "I live now, no longer I, but Christ lives in me" (*Gal.:* 2.20).

The word that is used for "spirit" and "spiritual" in the New Testament does not have the bleached out notion that the English words convey. In the original Greek, the words are "pneuma" and "pneumatic." These words convey something of the mystery and the paradoxical qualities of spirit.

In his treatise on the Holy Spirit, St. Basil describes some of these: "Simple in substance, manifold in powers, present entirely in each individual while existing in entirety everywhere, divided without suffering diminution, shared without loss of completeness... the Spirit comes to each of these who receive him, as though given to him alone; yet he sends out to all his grace, sufficient and complete, and all who partake in him receive benefit in proportion to the capacity, not of his power, but of their nature."

This theme of the transposition of the "Pneuma" of God, the Holy Spirit, into our own spirits is a theme that runs through the letters of Paul. In particular, Ch. 8 of Romans describes the contrast between the new personality of the Christian, that is, the "pneumatic person," and one who still lives on the level of what is simply human, the "unpneumatic person:" "Those who live on the level of our lower nature have their outlook formed by it, and that spells death; but those who live on the level of the Pneuma have the pneumatic outlook, and that is life and peace... But that is not how you live. You are on the pneumatic level, if only God's Pneuma dwells within you; and if a man does not possess the Pneuma of Christ, he is no Christian" (*Rm.:* 8.5,6,8,9).

To appreciate the meaning of spiritual direction, we have to recapture the Scriptural sense of the "pneumatic" person into whom the "Pneuma" of Christ has been transposed. In the second place, we have to situate the notion of "direction" into the direction which is given by the Spirit who has been poured into the Church and into the heart of each Christian.

The transposition of the Spirit into our spirits carries with it the transposition of the direction of the spirit into the natural direction of our spirits. This is another way of speaking of "teleology," or the inbuilt orientation to a goal. The Christian, then, takes on the orientation, direction, teleology of the Spirit. Again, in the words of St. Paul: "Everyone who is united to Christ is one Spirit with him" (1 *Co.:* 6.17). This means that a person united to Christ through the Spirit has the same inner direction as Christ and the Holy Spirit.

The Holy Spirit has only one orientation, that is, to create in us the image of Christ. Paul sees the action of the Spirit and that of Christ as having the same direction: "We all reflect as in a mirror the splendor of the Lord; thus we are transfigured into his likeness, from splendor to splendor; such is the influence of the Lord who is Spirit" (2 *Co.:* 3.18).

In the most profound sense the Holy Spirit is the spiritual director. It is he who orientates us most radically to our goal. All other forms of spiritual direction in the Church are only instrumental and derivative of the primary director and his direction. It also follows that the norm of the genuineness of spiritual direction as we ordinarily use the term has its base in the conformity of the human spirit to the Holy Spirit.

Spiritual direction, then, is the way that a person or institution fosters the life and the direction of the Holy Spirit, bringing the various aspects of a person's life into a convergence, freeing the person from whatever gets in the way of the direction of the Spirit in his life. All spiritual direction, in the human sense, lives in a kind of apprenticeship to the Holy Spirit. "We are God's work of art" (*Ep.:* 2.10), as Paul puts it. Human spiritual directors are in some way instruments or disciples of the main artist, the Holy Spirit. Like some of the famous painters who have a school of disciples, the Holy Spirit has many disciples who are engaged in one work of art, which is to change us into the image of Christ.

We speak of spiritual direction *in the Church.* It is important to see that the Holy Spirit is not simply given to the individual Christian as an isolated individual. The gift to the person lives in the context of the gift given to the community. The Holy Spirit dwells in the whole Church as in a temple, as well as in the heart of each Christian.

At this point, it will be helpful to recall some of the texts from the Constitution on the Church of Vatican II which highlight the role of the Spirit in the life of the Church. I shall not quote all of the texts, but enough of them to give a sense of the richness of the treatment.

> When the work which the Father gave the Son to do on earth was accomplished, the Holy Spirit was sent on the day of Pentecost in order that He might continually sanctify the Church and thus all those who believe would have access through Christ in Spirit to the Father. He is the Spirit of Life, a fount of water springing up to life eternal. To men, dead in sin, the Father gives life through Him; until, in Christ, He brings to life their mortal bodies. The Spirit dwells in the Church and in the hearts of the faithful, as in a Temple. In them He prays on their behalf and bears witness to the fact that they are adopted sons.

The Church, which the Spirit guides in way of all truth and which He unified in communion and in works of ministry, He both equips and directs with hierarchical and charismatic gifts and adorns with His fruits...

All members ought to be molded in the likeness of Him until Christ be formed in them... In order that we might be unceasingly renewed in Him, He has shared with us His Spirit who, existing as one and the same being in the Head and in the members, gives life to, unifies and moves through the whole body. This He does in such a way that His work could be compared by the Holy Fathers with the function which the principle of life, that is, the soul, fulfills in the human body (#7).

When we speak, then, of spiritual direction in the Church, we mean there is a divine, personal, vivifying, unifying, centering power directing both the Church as a whole and each member to the same goal. The Spirit is at work in the whole Church in order to provide the milieu for what he wants to accomplish in each individual, that is, the formation of Christ. Paul describes this goal: "...that the universe, all in heaven and on earth, might be brought into a unity in Christ" (*Ep.:* 1.10). In this sense, communion-creating love is the motivating power at the heart of reality, the love of Father for Son, the Son for the Father, and the Holy Spirit whose whole meaning as person is to transpose into mankind the communion which exists within the Trinity.

We have been using the term "transposition" to describe how this greater reality, namely, the orientating Spirit, is poured into us who are so limited. The Gospel of John describes the gift of the Spirit into the Church in language that is very much like that which we have been using. After his resurrection, Jesus appeared to his disciples. He said, "Peace be with you." Then he carries out the fulfillment of all that he came to do. He transposes the gift of his own mission into the Apostles by giving them his Spirit: " 'As the Father has sent me, so I send you.' He breathed on them, saying, 'Receive the Holy Spirit. If you forgive any man's sins, they stand forgiven. If you pronounce them unforgiven, unforgiven they remain' " (*Jn.:* 20. 19-23).

The words which Jesus uses recalls the words of Genesis: 2.7, which describe the mystery of the initial transposition of God's spirit into clay in order to form man. "Then he breathed into his nostrils a breath of life, and thus man became a living being." In both passages, there is a description of a transposition of the higher into the lower. In the account in John, Christ, first in symbolic gesture, the breathing on them, then in word, transposes into the Apostles his orientating Spirit, which is the transposition of his own mission into them.

We have spoken about spiritual direction in the Church by clarifying its uniqueness in the Christian sense compared with the practice of teacher-disciple relationship which exists among all peoples. We described this uniqueness in terms of transposition of Christ's directing Spirit into the Church. Hence, what we ordinarily call spiritual direction is always in service of the primary Spiritual

Director, the Holy Spirit.

Because of this transposition, spiritual direction takes on another aspect which makes it completely different from the ordinary human process by which people guide others. It is called by various names, the paschal mystery, the wisdom of the cross, renunciation. Paul speaks of the scandal of the cross as being the wisdom of God, but foolishness to the world (1 *Co.:*1). A spiritual director has to be aware of this mystery as it calls forth in the Christian this same foolishness of God. Each Christian is called to live this mystery in some way. Those called to the life of the evangelical counsels are to make an explicit profession of the paschal mystery in the life of chastity, poverty, obedience. The paschal mystery finds supreme manifestation in martyrdom.

The human spiritual director must be especially sensitive to the movements of the Holy Spirit. This involves a two-sided *sym-pathy*, that is, in the original meaning of the word, a feeling-with, that has reaches in two directions: the sympathy, or feeling with, that comes from sensitivity to the Spirit; and then, a feeling-with that comes from a sensitivity to the person he is directing. It is a sym-pathy that has its origin in the fact that they are animated by the same Holy Spirit. This sym-pathy creates a certain resonance between the spiritual director and the one whom he is directing. They are being moved in the same direction by the Holy Spirit. This movement takes a conscious shape in the sharing of a common faith, the same hopes, and the love that binds all together.

There is an imperative built into the orientation given to us by the Spirit. The human director has to sense the pressure of that imperative, and to bring it to fruition in the one whom he is directing. In the words of St. Paul, the imperative is to take on the identity of Christ: "Let this mind be in you which was in Christ Jesus" (*Ph.:*2.4). It is the imperative to allow the Holy Spirit to coordinate all of our activities to this one purpose: "If the Spirit is the source of our life, let the Spirit also direct our course" (*Gal.:*5.25).

There is, however, another important aspect of this spiritual sympathy. It gives the director a kind of spiritual smell for *evil*. In this sense evil is that which opposes the orientation of the Father as given to us in the Spirit of his Son. Evil, therefore, is always an attempt to block, suppress, or disorientate the orientation of the Spirit. Hence, there is need for discernment of spirits: "But do not trust any and every spirit, my friends; test the spirits, to see whether they are from God" (1 *Jn.:* 4.1).

The evil spirit can attempt to block the work of the Holy Spirit in many ways: by the simulation of what is good; by creating a state of soul that is confused, troubled, and distrubed by emotions contrary to the spirit, such as anger, resentment, pride, unforgiveness. Any disturbance of the fundamental peace which is the sign of the Spirit's presence can make discernment difficult. Perhaps the infallible sign of the presence of the evil spirit is not the antagonism to what is good, but to the paschal mystery itself, wherever that is incarnated. For this reason, the key temptation in the account of Jesus' temptation in the desert was aimed at blocking the paschal mystery itself.

This discernment, however, goes beyond the sense of the evil presence in the heart of individuals. It exists also on the whole stage in which the drama of human life is played out. St. Paul speaks of "cosmic powers, authorities, and potentates of this dark world, superhuman forces of evil in the heavens" (*Ep.*: 6.12). These evil influences are more difficult to detect because the pressure of their presence is not noticed. What is simply part of the furniture of our world is hardly noticed. It is like a person living in a room where the air is stale. He does not notice it. Only a person who comes in out of the fresh air can discern how stale the air is.

The nature of the evil powers is to block the orientation of the Spirit and to narrow the consciousness of individuals to the point where there is fixation on only one narrow aspect. The Prince of this World, as Jesus called him, captured Judas by narrowing his consciousness to what he could get from betraying Christ. As C.S. Lewis has his character Screwtape say: "Humans think we tempt them by putting thoughts in their mind. They don't realize that we tempt them by keeping thoughts out of their mind."

In the Apocalypse, John describes how the evil powers, in a kind of diabolical imitation of the Holy Spirit, enlist others in their work: e.g., the Roman emperors and the pagan priesthood in an effort to crush the Church. One of the important aspects of spiritual direction, then, is to be able to detect the presence of evil, not only in an individual, but also on a societal level. On such a level it presents an anti-milieu to what Teilhard de Chardin speaks of as "the divine milieu."

2. The Practice of Spiritual Direction: Its Foundation

On the foundational level, Jesus Christ is the fullest expression of the orientation of the Spirit. He is fullness of what we speak of as a "spiritual director." In addition, there are the apostles and evangelists. Among these St. Paul is preeminent. Thirdly, there is the practice of spiritual direction which grew up with many variations in the history of the Church. We shall take up these different modes of instrumentation in the following pages.

It is important to realize that spiritual direction is not only that which takes place between individuals but also that which takes place between institutions and persons. It is the institution which provides the "milieu" in which the direction is taking place. It sets the basic norms for spiritual direction by providing the "coordinates," so to speak, on which it all takes place. This is what St. Paul speaks of as "healthy doctrine." Spiritual direction by its very nature presupposes that one is operating out of revealed truth. There is not much value in setting a ship in order if it is off the course and headed in the wrong direction.

Let us, then, reflect on Christ as the spiritual director in the primary sense. Of course, when speaking of Jesus as "spiritual director," we have to expand our ordinary understanding of the term.

In the first place, Jesus is the one who has made spiritual direction in any sense of the term possible. He is the one who by reconciling us to the Father through his redemptive act has redirected us to the Father. It is he who has endowed us with the gift of the Spirit who serves as the redirection power of Christ within us. In this primary sense, Christ is spiritual director in reorientating the whole of creation to the Father.

But, in the second place, Jesus himself who is filled with the Spirit is one who through his teaching guides us to the Father. The one who listens to his words is listening to the words which the Father has given him: "The one whom God has sent speaks the words of God" (*Jn.:* 3.24). "I myself am not the source of the words I speak to you" (*Jn.:* 14.10). His words are to free us and fill us with life: "The words I spoke to you are spirit and life" (*Jn.:* 6.33). The Spirit who descends upon him at the time of his baptism is the orientating power of the Father. All that Jesus does comes from a sensitivity to the holy pressure of the Spirit.

While Jesus is the spiritual director in all that he does and says, we find in the discourse of Jesus at the Last Supper, as described in the Gospel of John, a beautiful model of spiritual direction in his dialogue with the apostles. I would like to comment on this discourse briefly.

First of all, Jesus has the kind of sym-pathy that we spoke of above. He is "on the side of" the Spirit, and "on the side of" the apostles. Being on the side of the Spirit, in a most wondrous way he can describe the very characteristics of the Spirit. The way that he describes the Holy Spirit shows that he is in someway identified with the Spirit. He can read his mind, his heart, and his role, because there is a kind of spiritual resonance between Spirit and Son.

He describes the Spirit as another advocate (counselor, consoler): "I will ask the Father and he will give you another Advocate, who will be with you forever, the Spirit of truth" (*Jn.:* 13.15). The Holy Spirit is a teacher, who continues to expand the teaching of Jesus himself: "The Holy Spirit whom the Father will send in my name will teach you everything, and will call to mind all that I have told you" (*Jn.:* 14.26).

He will bear witness to Jesus. This means that he will be the verification of Jesus' own life and teaching: "But when your Advocate has come, whom I will send you from the father -- the Spirit of truth that issues from the Father -- he will bear witness to me" (*Jn.:* 15.26).

He will also disclose the hearts of people, show (to use our current expression) where "people are coming from." "He will confute the world, and show where wrong and right and judgment lie" (*Jn.:* 16.7). The Holy Spirit discloses what is in the human heart. In particular, he discloses how all sin is in someway a rejection of Christ himself.

The Holy Spirit will become the guide when Jesus goes to the Father. He will be the "spiritual director." He will direct the Apostles and the Church to all truth. During the time before his Second Coming, he will unfold the richness of the truth that is in Christ: "He will guide you into all truth... everything that he makes known to you he will draw from me" (*Jn.:* 16.15). The Holy Spirit, then, is the primary spiritual director, who draws all the content of the direction from Christ, and, in his own proper role, orientates all things. especially the Church and its members, to forming the full stature of Christ: "So shall we all at last attain to the unity inherent in our faith and our knowledge of the Son of God -- to mature manhood, measured by nothing less than the full stature of Christ" (*Ep.:* 4.13).

Jesus is not only on the "inside" of the Spirit to the point where he can draw the "profile" of the Spirit but he also exhibits those characteristics in his way of directing the apostles: "Set your troubled hearts are rest. Trust in God always. Trust also in me. There are many dwelling places in my Father's house. If it were not so, I should have told you; for I am going there on purpose to prepare a place for you. And if I go and prepare a place for you, I shall come again and receive you to myself, so that where I am you also may be" (*Jn.:* 14. 1-3).

He is "on the inside" of the apostles. He knows his sheep by name, and calls them by name. He reads their hearts, senses their fears, repeatedly assures them that he is not going to leave them orphans, but that he will come to be with them in a deeper way, through the gift of his spirit.

He teaches them the truth about himself: he is the Way, the Truth, and the Life. He teaches them the truth about the Father: "This is eternal life to know thee, the only true God, and him whom you have sent" (*Jn.:* 17. 3). He exposes the power of evil at work in the world, and assures them that the power of the Prince of this world is about to be broken. He senses the presence of that Prince of darkness in the presence of one who is to betray him. When they need him most, after they had betrayed him, he seeks them out. In particular, he seeks out Peter, and, as spiritual director, tells him that he himself will walk the path of the paschal mystery.

It would be possible to go through all of the Gospels from this particular point of view to see how Jesus is the spiritual director. We find in him in a paradigmatic way the meaning of spiritual direction and the qualities of a spiritual director. Coming in touch with him is coming into a *presence*. An individual senses that he is in the presence of someone to whom he cannot be indifferent. Jesus discloses the heart of each person and draws him to a new level in his relationship to the Father. Not content with observance of the commandments, Jesus attracts his people to the "more" of his paschal mystery: "If you want to go the whole way, go; sell your possessions; give to the poor; and then you will have riches in heaven; and come, follow me" (*Mt.:* 19. 21). "While some are incapable of marriage because they were born so, or were made so by men, there are others who have themselves renounced marriage for the sake of the kingdom of Heaven. Let those accept it who can" (*Mt.:* 19. 22).

We turn, then, to the letters of Paul to comment briefly on how he himself fulfills his role as a spiritual director. In his letters to Philemon, Timothy, Titus, we find the person-to-person direction which is aimed at leading each of them to a fuller realization of their faith and a more fruitful apostolate.

I spoke about the "sym-pathy" that should characterize the spiritual director. Paul's letters are filled with this sense of identity with his flock: "I am all things to all men to win all to Christ" (1 *Co.:* 9. 22). "Who is weak and I am not weak" (2 *Co.:* 11. 29). "We were gentle as a nurse caring fondly for her children" (1 *Th.:* 2. 7). "As you well know, we dealt with you one by one, as a father deals with his children, appealing to you by encouragement, as well as by solemn injunctions, to live lives worthy of the God who calls you into his kingdom and glory" (1 *Th.:* 2. 11, 12).

In his letter to Timothy, he stresses the foundation of all spiritual direction: *truth.* For Paul, truth is not an abstraction. It is the Gospel entrusted to him by Jesus Christ: "If anyone preaches a gospel at variance with the gospel which you received, let him be outcast" (*Gal.:* 1. 9). In the letters to Timothy he coins a phrase to show the relationship between the gospel and one's life: "healthy doctrine," "healthy teaching." "This is what you are to teach and preach. If anyone is teaching otherwise, and will not give his mind to healthy teaching -- I mean those of our Lord Jesus Christ -- and to good religious teaching, I call him a pompous ignoramus" (1 *Tm.:* 6. 3). "The time will come when they will not stand wholesome teaching, but will be avid for the latest novelty and collect for themselves a whole series of teachers according to their own tastes" (2 *Tm.:* 4. 3).

This doctrine is not something he or any human being invented, but it is a sacred trust given to the Church by Christ. Paul writes:

"Timothy, keep safe that which has been entrusted to you" (1 *Tm.:* 6. 20). "Keep as your pattern the sound teaching you have heard from me, in the faith and love that are in Christ Jesus. You have been trusted to look after something precious; guard it with the help of the Holy Spirit who lives in us" (2 *Tm.:* 1. 13, 14). "Put that teaching into the charge of men you can trust, such men as will be competent to teach others" (2 *Tm.:* 2. 2). "They must be men who combine a clear conscience with a firm hold on the deep mystery of our faith" (1 *Tm.:* 2. 9).

The preservation of "healty doctrine" is not left to the vagaries of history. It finds its protection and foundation in the Church, which is "God's household, the Church of the living God, which upholds the truth and keeps it safe" (1 *Tm.:* 3. 14, 15).

The letter to Philemon which consists of only twenty-five verses is a kind of mini-course in spiritual direction. He teaches Philemon how he should face a painful situation in a truly Christian way. Philemon's slave, Onesimus, had run away, and come in contact with Paul, who baptized him. Now Paul sends him back with following advice to his owner: "I am sending him back to you... no longer as a slave, but as more than a slave -- as a dear brother, very dear indeed to me and how much dearer to you, both as man and as Christian" (12, 16).

It seems to me that the spiritual genius of Paul lies in the instinctive way in which he can rise from a particular situation to the larger mystery, and draw the application from the larger mystery to the particular case. For example, he teaches the Corinthians that fornication is a desecration not only of their own bodies but of Christ himself, i.e. by recalling the mystery of the identity of the Christian, anyone united to Christ is "one spirit with him" (1 *Co.:* 6. 17). To teach the lesson of humility, he rises to the mystery of the "lowering" of Christ to take on our human nature, and even the death of a criminal (*Ph.:* 2. 12). This pattern of making a judgment about the particular through a sense of the implications involved in the Christian mysteries is of the essence of spiritual direction.

Finally, another characteristic of the spiritual director is always at work in Paul. It is the sense of the inbuilt movement of the Spirit toward the "more" of the spiritual life: "Finally, brothers, we urge you and appeal to you in the Lord Jesus to make more and more progress in the kind of life that you are meant to live" (1 *Th.:* 4. 1). He compares the "more" of the spiritual life with an abundant harvest we are to cultivate (*Gal.:* 5. 22). If our lives have a genuine direction, then we are being progressively transformed into the image of Christ: "We all reflect as in a mirror the splendor of the Lord; thus we are transfigured into his likeness, from splendor to splendor. Such is the influence of mount and overflow towards one another and towards all, as our love mount and overflow towards one another and towards all, as our live does towards you" (1 *Th.:* 3. 11, 12).

3. The Practice of Spiritual Direction: Its History

We come to the practice of spiritual direction in the history of the Church, after which we will take up some ideas on spiritual direction in the Church today. Usually any discussion of spiritual direction begins with these themes. In our treatment they come at the end. They do not make sense unless we understand, in the first place, that Christ is the one who has redirected us to the Father through his redemptive act, and that he continues this direction through the gift of his Spirit; secondly, that Christ and his apostles also show in practice the meaning of spiritual direction. The practice of spiritual direction in the Church has certain invariable qualities found at every point of history; on the other hand, it will also assume different "styles" according to various historical circumstances. I can only comment briefly on the practices found over a period of nearly 2000 years in the Church.

The practice of spiritual direction comes into its own as a teacher-disciple relationship in the fourth century with the emergence of the monastic life. Thomas Merton describes this period very well: "It must not be forgotten that the spiritual director in primitive times was much more than the present name implies. He was a spiritual father who 'begot' the perfect life in the soul of his disciple by his instructions first of all, but also by his prayer, his sanctity and his example. He was to the young monk a kind of 'sacrament' of the Lord's presence in the ecclesiastical community" (from *Writings on Spiritual Direction*, Neufelder and Coelho, eds., Seabury: 1982).

The practice of spiritual direction at this stage strikes us as very different from what goes by that name today. In the direction that was given, there was a sense of the prophetic word that would resonate with the inner spirit of the person to achieve what the person needed -- encouragement, advice, exhortation, correction, etc. But the constant was there, the sym-pathia of the director with the Holy Spirit and with the spirit of the disciple.

It seems that subsequently the "prophetic" nature of this relationship was attenuated from what might be described as an apodictic form to one that was more along the lines of pointing out to a person the direction he should take. Perhaps we could say that "hieratic" was succeded by the "prudential" mode. I hope that this is a legitimate way of generalizing the kind of change that took place from the erly monastic form to that which became customary in Benedictine spirituality, and in the general practice of the Church.

To attempt to describe the practice of spiritual direction in the Church over a period of fifteen centuries would entail a commentary on practically all of the saints. It is no exaggeration to say that all of the great saints, men, women, priests, religious, and lay were spiritual directors. (For an exhaustive treatment, see "Direction Spirituelle," in

Dictionnaire de Spiritualite). One of the common ways in which this was carried out was through letters. Augustine, for example, has scores of letters which have as their explicit purpose spiritual direction.

St. Ignatius of Loyola holds a special place in the history of the Church. We recall how he had been wounded in battle, and during the course of his convalescence, while reading the lives of the saints, he underwent an experience of conversion. After he recovered, he went to Manresa where he spent a year in prayer and penance. During this time, except for the direction given by his confessor, he had no spiritual director. Nevertheless, he was directed by God: "At this time, God treated him just as a schoolmaster treats a little boy when he teaches him. This was perhaps because of his rough and uncultivated understanding, or because he had no one to teach him, or because of the firm will God Himself had given him in His service. But he clearly saw, and always had seen that God dealt with him like this" (*Ignatius' Own Story*, William Young, S.J., Loyola University Press, 1956, p. 22).

During his stay in Manresa, he began to direct others: "Besides his seven hours of prayer, he busied himself with certain souls who came looking for him to discuss their spiritual interests" (*Ibid.*, p. 21). The special gift of the Spirit to Ignatius was to see how the Lord was directing him. He discovered the Spirit's direction through discerning the direction of desires within his own spirit: where they came from, where they were going, and how they affected his own interior disposition. Desires fro the Holy Spirit affected his own spirit in a vastly different way than desires prompted by the evil spirit or from his own natural instincts.

Ignatius' own experience and the way that he embodied that experience in the *Spiritual Exercises* gave him a particular orientation to directing others. The distinctive "components" of spiritual direction began to take on their own identity, together with the sense of a symphonic whole. He saw that spiritual direction aims at freeing oneself from whatever gets in the way of doing God's will: "For every one must keep in mind that in all that concerns the spiritual life his progress will be in proportion to his surrender of self-love and of his own will and interests" (*Sp. Ex.* #189). The process of discernment is essential, and presupposes that the one being directed has opened his heart completely to the director.

There is stress on daily examination of conscience, not so much to see how a person has succeeded or failed, but to look at the "confluence" where the movements of the Holy Spirit in our spirit during the day met in a kind of confluence with the daily circumstances of our lives. Then to reflect whether the direction this "confluence" took was marked by the direction of the Spirit or not.

Spiritual direction, then, should aim at drawing a person to the *magis* in the service of Christ, the *greater* glory of God. In the *Spiritual Exercises* this *magis* is put before the retreatant at key moments: in the meditation on the call of Christ the King, and in the reflection on the Third Mode of Humility. In each of these, the retreatant is invited to offer his life to assume the paschal mode of Christ's own life, and to serve Christ and the Church in a redemptive mode of life.

To preserve a person from spirituality that is myoptic and thus in danger of distortion, St Ignatius stresses the need of guidance from the Church: "We must put aside all judgment of our own, and keep the mind ever ready and prompt to obey in all things the true Spouse of Christ our Lord, our holy Mother, the hierarchical Church" (*Sp. Ex.* 353).

It can safely be said that God's gift to the Church through Ignatius was to provide a spiritual "milieu" in which direction would take place, namely, the *Spiritual Exercises*. In the spiritual exercises, the role of the spiritual director became more "formalized," that is, it began to be differentiated from other aspects of pastoral care.

4. Spiritual Direction in the Church Today

I think that this process of the "formalization" of spiritual direction has entered a new phase within the past twenty years. Perhaps it is only following the laws at work in every area of human experience: the movement toward differentiation and specialization. There has been more written on the specific topic of spiritual direction in the past twenty years than was written over all of the previous centuries in the history of the Church. Along the same lines, for the first time in history, scores of programs have been set up with the explicit goal to equip people to give spiritual direction.

There has also been a kind of "raising of consciousness" for the need of spiritual direction, not only for priests and religious, but also for the laity. In fact, we are caught in a situation where the demand is vastly out of proportion with the supply of good spiritual directors.

The retreat houses across the country are enjoying an unprecedented volume of retreatants, making everything from weekend to thirty day retreats, both group retreats, and private directed retreats. The practice of "at home" retreats, or, in the Ignatian terminology, "Nineteenth Annotation retreats," is growing at a phenomenal rate. Spiritual direction is one of the main activities during these retreats.

Before I try to assess what is happening here, I want to step back to the directives given in Vatican II for training priests in spiritual direction: "Spiritual formation should be closely linked with doctrinal and pastoral training. Especially with the help of the spiritual director, such formation should help seminarians learn to live in familiar and constant companionship with the Father, through Jesus Christ His Son, in the Holy Spirit" (*Decree on Priestly Formation* #8). "Let them receive careful instruction in the art of guiding souls, so that they can lead all sons of the Church, before everything else, to a Christian life which is fully conscious and apostolic, and to fulfillment of the duties of their state. With equal thoroughness they should learn to assist men and women religious to persevere in the grace of their vocation and to make progress according to the spirit of their various communities" (#19).

It seems to me that the growing awareness of the need for spiritual direction is one of the signs of the hunger felt for a deeper relationship with God. This movement is not loud and ostentatious. It belongs on the level of the silent springs that water the world through expanding the spirit. These are not the kind of activities that hit the media. But they are definitely signs of the movement of the Holy Spirit.

But who are these people directing and being directed? By that question I am not asking about the kind of groups into which they can be broken down: lay, religious, priest. They are different people from those who have gone ahead of us in previous centuries. Their attitudes have been shaped not only by what took place during those centuries, such as the Renaissance, the Enlightenment but also by more recent developments in psychology and sociology. There is no doubt that the knowledge of these disciplines can help a director and the one he is directing. At the same time, a subtle "reality shift" can take place. The things of the spirit tend to take on a lesser reality, while the principles of psychology and sociology become more real and more effective. They are, in fact, easier to get a handle on, while the things of the spirit are not under our control. Unconsciously, then, the weight of attention tends to shift from the spirit to the concreteness offered by psychology and sociology. The sense of the ontological roots of spiritual direction, the presence of the Holy Spirit who is poured into our hearts, can be attenuated and lost in the face of the apparent impact of psychological and sociological realities.

There are also pervasive moods that are in the air. Without our being aware of them, they form the optic through which we see reality. One of these is what is called humanistic psychology. It is really not psychology. It is a thinly disguised philosophy of human nature. Its basic assumption is that we are all naturally good. According to this position, what we call evil is merely some kind of a defect like that which makes a tree crooked. A tree can be straightened out by "tree therapy." Human nature, if it is warped, can also be straightened out by various techniques. Underlying this humanistic psychology is the assumption that our human nature is not in need of redemption. Whatever is wrong can be cured by the therapy of interpersonal dynamics.

However, in the Christian view, what was and is wrong with human nature cannot be set right by any amount of human effort. This is what is meant by the redemption. While the Holy Spirit is the source of life on every level, even tree-life, he is the source of the spiritual life only by inserting us into the one who died and rose. That is the therapy of the Holy Spirit. It is possible that the prevalence of the view of human existence that comes from a humanistic psychology can dim out the need for this spiritual therapy.

Perhaps no person giving spiritual direction would subscribe to this humanistic philosophy of human nature. On the other hand, the attitude is so pervasive that it can imperceptibly color a person's attitude and affect his approach to spiritual direction.

Another pervasive mood is a secularistic mentality which filters out the sense of the sacred in the world. It is particularly harmful if the sense of the sacred is not present in the context of spiritual direction. It is possible to talk of spiritual things, and even give spiritual direction without the sense of the sacred. But we must adapt the words of St. Paul: "If I am without a sense of the Spirit, I am a sounding gong or a clanging cymbal" (1 *Co.:* 13. 1). We must attempt to recapture the "hieratic" sense, the sense of the holy, which Merton describes as the vital context of spiritual direction in the early Church. In this content, the director became "a sacrament" of the Lord's presence in the ecclesiastical community.

We are back once more to the fundamental meaning of spiritual direction, which is the human effort to channel the movement of the Holy Spirit to bring about a deeper orientation of a person to the Father. Such an awareness disposes us to the fundamental disposition of the director and one being directed. This is *docility.* Literally, this means "teachability." We are alerted to this need for docility to the Spirit when we consciously attempt to put ourselves in the milieu of the sacred.

I think that we are living at a special time in history. As is true of any special manifestation of the Spirit in history, we stand on the shoulders of those who have gone before us. At the same time, we are in the presence of the freedom and unpredictability of the Spirit who "lists where he will." No one could have dreamed of this development twenty-five years ago. Where this is going and what it is preparing the Church for lies hidden in the designs of the Director of directors: the Holy Spirit.

Conclusion

I would like to conclude by giving a description of what is meant by spiritual direction.

In first place, it is direction transposed into the Church and into individuals by the Holy Spirit. He is the primary director. In Christ we find the paradigm of spiritual direction. He himself through his openness to the direction of the Spirit was obedient to the Father's will which issued in his sacrificial death. He transposed his own mission and orientation into the apostles through the gift of the Spirit.

In the letters of St. Paul we find the characteristics of a spiritual director who is sensitive to the movement of the Spirit. Throughout the history of the Church, the Holy Spirit has worked through thousands of directors to draw others into the direction of the Spirit.

Spiritual direction has many forms. But the constant in each of them is sensitivity to the primary spiritual director, the Holy Spirit. There are as many ways of spiritual direction as there are ways in which the Spirit orientates us to Christ and to the Father: through institutions like the Church and religious orders; the Christian family; parents; the Gospel; homilies; sacraments; the example of others. We should be mindful, then, of the immense amount of spiritual direction we already have through our common spiritual heritage. This should be reassuring when we think it hard to find a personal director.

As the term is ordinarily used, a spiritual director is one, who through the power and wisdom of the Spirit, acts as a spiritual guide for a person over a significant period of time. Through a kind of spiritual artistry, he attempts to bring about a convergence of the whole person to the master-vision of faith, and a master-commitment to Christ. The words of St. Paul can be applied to this process of spiritual artistry: "I am in labor with you over again until Christ is formed in you" (*Gal.:* 4. 19).

I spoke of "sym-pathy" as being one of the characteristics of the spiritual director. I shall end this long paper with a story about one of the desert fathers from the fourth century: "Some old men came to see Abba Poemen and said to him, 'When we see brothers who are dozing at the common prayer, shall we wake them so that they will be attentive?' He said to them, 'When I personally see a brother who is nodding in sleep, I put his head on my knees and let him be at peace.'"

Response to Father Sheets
by
Msgr. John P. McIvor

Father Sheets began his talk by focusing on what is unique and specific about spiritual direction in the Church. He spoke about the mystery of the Holy Spirit being poured forth into the hearts of the faithful, a mystery which changes us and makes us "pneumatic" or spirit-filled people. He emphasized that the spiritual director "par excellence" is the Holy Spirit who is creating us anew, inspiring us and enabling us to relive the paschal mystery of Christ. Father Sheets stressed the fact that spiritual directors in the Church must be sensitive to and appreciative of this mystery of the indwelling of the Spirit, and that they themselves must become spirit-filled if they are to guide others in living out this mystery.

I found Father Sheet's treatment of St. Paul especially inspiring. St. Paul more than anyone else in the New Testament manifests the qualities of what a good spiritual director should be. Father Sheets speaks about Paul's spiritual genius and his ability to size up a particular situation and relate it to the mystery of our being new creatures in Christ, temples of His Spirit, members of His Body. Paul has, says Father Sheets "...a sense of the inbuilt imperative of the life of the Holy Spirit to grow, to reach out and to expand to the utmost." The Spirit challenges us to be more and to do more in terms of our commitment to Christ in the context of our particular state in life.

I would like to elaborate on this genius of St. Paul's. He is intent on making his directees aware of the mystery of Christ in them. He uses the phrases, "In Christ" or "Christ in us," more than 165 times, as well as the phrase, "Body of Christ," to impress upon his listeners, his disciples, the mystery of who and what they are. Father Fitzmyer writes in the *JBC*: "Christian existence for Paul is not merely an existence dominated by new psychological motivation, but rather is the reshaping of man's very physical life by the transcendent influence of Christ's indwelling." For Paul, faith in Christ "...reshapes man anew internally, supplying him with a new principle of activity on the ontological level of his very being. A symbiosis results of man with Christ, the glorified 'Kyrios' who has become by the resurrection a 'vivifying spirit,' (1 *Cor.:* 15:45), the vital spirit of Christian activity." (*JBC*, "Letter to the Galatians" p. 244)

Having impressed his listeners on who they are, Paul challenges them to be what they claim to be. He constantly reminds them that in a certain transhistorical sense they are already redeemed, that they are mystically identified with Christ in the saving mystery of His cross and resurrection. However, at the same time he exhorts them in their present historical situation and circumstances of life to strive to relive and assimilate the sacred events of Christ's life. In other words, their mystical identification must be translated into moral action. Paul writes: "If you have risen with Christ seek the things that are above." (*Col.:* 3: 1)

We find, then that the depth of the richness of Paul's understanding of the Christian's relationship to Christ and the indwelling of the Holy Spirit is paralleled by a spirituality or an ethics in Paul which challenges and demands that the Christian be what he already is, that is, a new man delivered from the domination of sin and transformed by Christ into a new existence. (*Romans:* 6:14) Paul is intent on making his readers aware of both what has been done for them in Christ and what is now expected of them. As you read St. Paul, therefore, you notice that his emphasis on the Holy Spirit is also accompanied by a corresponding number of norms, precepts and principles which are meant to govern the Christian's moral life. He often lists a number of virtues which are expected of the Christian with the vices which are to be avoided. These mark, at least, the boundaries of what is expected and not expected of one who claims to be "in Christ."

Father Sheets speaks a great deal about "pneuma" or the Holy Spirit in his paper and rightly so. I would like to focus for a few moments on another reality which Paul often juxtaposes to that of "Spirit" or "pneuma." It is the reality of "sarx" or "flesh." On the one hand, Paul speaks of the person who lives "with and in Christ" as belonging to that mode or sphere of existence which he calls "pneuma." Such a person has power over sin and belongs to the new order of things. On the other hand, Paul speaks of the person who lives without Christ as belonging to that mode or sphere of existence which he calls "sarx." Such a person is under the power of sin and belongs to the old order of things. His manner of existence is oriented to the visible, to the tangible, and to the exclusion of God.

The word "sarx" for Paul stands for everything that is natural, physical, visible, weak and earthbound in man. It connotes the natural human creature left to himself. At the same time, Paul teaches that the person who is in Christ and lives with Christ is always open to the possibility of falling under the influence of sarx. As long as man is present in this world, his redemption is incomplete. He is still eagerly awaiting the fullness of his redemption: the resurrection of his body. While he awaits this fullness, he remains within the sphere of "sarx," with its lusts and its passions (*Gal.:* 5:16). While his new life is hidden with God in Christ, the power of sin is still visible and effectively seeking to establish its rule over him. "The New Man," therefore, lives in a state of tension. He is still temporarily surrounded by the old eon or age (*Gal.:* 1:14; *Romans:* 12:2; 1 *Col.:* 3:18). He stands between the ages, between the pull of the flesh and the pull of the spirit, as he awaits the complete redemption of his body in the final resurrection. This state of incompleteness and the perduring state of tension that accompanies it leaves him open to the possibility of living according to the "flesh" rather than according to the Spirit. This fact leads Paul to draw on a wide variety of traditional moral knowledge both secular and religious, including the sayings of the Lord, to indicate what is expected and not expected of the person who claims to be in Christ.

Paul uses moral precepts or commandments to correct the disorders of those Christians who have succumbed to the promptings of the "flesh" and who no longer live according to the Spirit. At the same time, for those who are living by the Spirit, precepts and commandments are also necessary. They are meant to guide the Christian in his knowledge of what is expected of his new life in Christ.

Even though the indwelling of the Holy Spirit is primary and must be respected and emphasized, there is also a need for a moral wisdom or direction coming from outside of the believer. It is necessary in order that one might clearly distinguish the promptings of the Spirit from the promptings of the flesh. Fr. Lyonnet in his book *The Christian Lives by the Spirit* comments on this use of a direction or a law coming from outside of the believer: "The law is not without utility even for the just. Although he is in the state of grace, that is led by the Holy Spirit, the Christian for as long as he remains on earth possesses the spirit imperfectly, as a sort of pledge. (Cf. *Romans* 8:23; *2 Cor.:* 1:22). As long as he lives in a mortal body, he is never so completely freed from sin and from the flesh that he cannot at any moment fall back under their domination. Now, in this unstable situation, the external written law, the objective norm of man's moral conduct, will help his conscience which is so easily clouded by his passions; for the flesh continues to struggle against the Spirit. (Cf. *Gal.:* 5:17). The external written law will aid the individual to distinguish unerringly the works of the flesh from the fruit of the Spirit and not to confuse the inclinations of his own sin wounded nature with the inner promptings of the Spirit." ("Christian Freedom and The Law of the Spirit according to St. Paul," in *The Christian Lives by the Spirit,* p. 165).

Spiritual Life in the Family
by
Dr. Ronda Chervin

Whereas in times past the very title of this lecture would have called up a very clear idea of the subject matter, since Vatican II a great variety of images come to mind: many of them seemingly contradictory. Before Vatican II, the model for family spirituality was the type of life to be found in the family of St. Therese of Lisieux. After Vatican II, however, there was a tendency to down-grade the spirituality of sacrifice (popularly expressed in the phrase "offer everything up") in favor of such "incarnational" motifs as "my work is my prayer." There was an attempt to get away from so-called monastic spiritualities in order to discover ways of meeting Christ in the midst of family life through greater dialogue among wives and husbands and the sharing of thoughts and feelings with children. For this reason, rote methods of prayer were discouraged and replaced with more spontaneous modes or by individual paths. Those concerned with social justice were eager to show that their family life reflected gospel values in attitudes toward money, hospitality, service and politics. At the same time, perhaps as a balance, some families became intensely involved in charismatic prayer styles and contemplative prayer experience.

Presently there is a crisis in family spirituality which, I believe, is caused by the evident loss of spirituality among the young. Loss of faith has many causes: the most prominent being the lack of accountability created by the suppression of the doctrine of hell in a great deal of contemporary catechesis. "The fear of the Lord," as scripture says, "is the beginning of wisdom." Many young people lack awe because Jesus is to them not the Lord but a warm and complacent friend. Liturgies which are cozy but lacking in reverence surely have had an effect here. The alarming decadence of society as a whole makes it imperative that Christian youth be non-conforming, which is very painful and, at the same time, almost impossible to boys and girls who are influenced by hedonistic affluence into thinking that sacrifice is unthinkable.

What has been the reaction of parents to this crisis? Some have simply succumbed to the idea that a "God and Mammon" existence is the best that can be expected: they leave their kids alone and offer up their anguish as best they can. Others consider the climate to be so contrary to Catholic values that they have withdrawn their families from immersion in the culture by means of building up counter-culture communities such as chasrismatic covenant groups, strong third order communes such as the Dominican pro-life St. Martin de Porres Community, Marian groups such as the Immaculata, and others. It would take too long to mention them all. Most devout Catholics, however, are trying to go back to the fundamentals, while retaining some positive features of post-Vatican II developments. Since this group includes the majority of our serious Catholic family members, it is important to sketch out some of the elements of the spiritual life that is desirable for them on the basis of principles from the perennial teachings of the Church on spirituality of the family.

A key point I would like to emphasize here is that the vertical and the horizontal are held together in Catholic spirituality. A family person is not a monk or a nun, but is also clearly called to perfection. In spite of loud outcries to the contrary, there are no second-class citizens in the Church. The Gospel is for all. The call to holiness is for all (*Lumen Gentium*, 39).

Some elements of the spiritual path of family people may be outlined as follows:

(1) Sexuality and married life is willed by God as a good in spite of the brokenness we all have because of original and personal sin (*Familiaris Consortio*).

(2) The love of spouses for each other and for their children is an end in itself in the image of the Trinity. It is not simply a backdrop for the pursuit of self-fulfillment in careers (the most wonderfully expressed exposition of this theme can be found in Von Hildebrand's *Marriage*).

(3) The sacrifices involved in laying down one's life for others on a 24 hour basis constitute a deeply meaningful way of living out the Gospel.

(4) We image God in our work and leisure as we appreciate and build up basic goods: physical, emotional, and spiritual. This theme is wonderfully expressed in Pope John Paul II's *Covenant of Love*.

(5) The family is called to a "simple and austere life-style" (*Laborem Exercens*). This life style is open to the needs of others.

(6) We are called to reflect God's merciful love in our daily forgiveness of each other.

These "horizontal" elements of Christian family life must not be seen as separate from the life of prayerful communion with God, especially family rosary. They are to be infused with prayers of thanksgiving, praise, and self-offering. It would be desirable that families be given more teaching and exhortation towards these goals from the pulpit. Many family Catholics have come to realize that commitment to the values just outlined cannot come to fruition without a personal "vertical" spirituality as intense as that of any single or consecrated person.

Without a life in the sacraments (preferable daily) and of prayer-times long enough to overcome peaceless frenetic activism, we find ourselves losing heart. Symptoms of false resignation or despair include boredom, indifference, compulsive fantasies of escape, addiction to sinful escapes, coldness, and chronic uncontrollable interior or exterior anger. I believe that, unless we not only *believe* that our true home is heaven and that our deepest longings will be fulfilled in a supernatural manner but also *experience* foretastes of Christ's promises in prayer and in response to the beauty and goodness already ours on earth, we are bound to become discouraged. To overcome the temptation to melancholy, rage, or bleakness, we need to find ways to surround ourselves within the family and also in parish groups with the foretastes of heaven which can be found in prayer, in the healing ministry, in taking in the wisdom of the saints past and present through spiritual reading, and in Christian music and art. In this way the spiritual joy of the parents, amidst the normal and more terrible crosses of life, will make clear the way for the children. As Christopher Derrick is fond of saying, "Even if the children stray, they will know the way home."

Of course, the great commandment "to love God with your whole strength, and your neighbor as yourself" beautifully lays out for us how the vertical and horizontal thrust fit together. Since heaven is not to be a "solo-trip," but an experience of ineffable joy in the community of the faithful with our blessed Lord at the center, it is no good cultivating an isolated transcendent spirituality -- what used to be called by older writers "a false spirituality." The family state of life almost forces us off such a path, for how many contemporary children will readily allow their parents even 15 minutes of uninterrupted solitude! On the other hand, since eternity is not an earthly utopian community, it is equally false to develop love of neighbor without an intimate relationship to God as our first and infinite love.

Finally, for the Catholic, the family is never an isolated unit. We struggle and rejoice in the company of the other families in the parish with whom we should be ever more closely united and with our heavenly family, including Mary and Joseph, all the saints, our guardian angels, and the very source of our being, redemption, and sanctification: the Holy Trinity. "Sursum corda" -- let us lift up our hearts!

Response by Kevin Perrotta

Professor Chervin has offered us an excellent summary of principles of Christian family life. We could only wish that she had more time to develop her sketch of the family as a primary social sphere in which divine grace restores fallen human nature, training both spouses and children in a life of commitment, forgiveness, sacrifice, service to others, and the ordered pursuit of natural human goods.

Professor Chervin is keenly aware of the cultural conflict over these values of Christian family life. This conflict between the Christian spiritual vision of family life and the outlook of secular culture deserves emphasis. Professor Chervin says: "The alarming decadence of society as a whole makes it imperative that Christian youth be nonconforming, which is very painful, and, at the same time, almost impossible to boys and girls who are influenced by hedonistic affluence into thinking that sacrifice in unthinkable."

Indeed, the call to nonconformity *is* "imperative," but nevertheless for many Catholics, young and old, it has become "unthinkable." Declining to pay the price of nonconformity, Catholic families have plunged themselves into the contemporary American crisis of family life.

Two developments illustrate the seriousness of the crisis ina particularly striking way.

First, Catholic marriages are collapsing at a remarkable rate. Social survey findings, compiled by the National Opinion Research Center and analyzed by the Roper organization, show that between 1972-73 and 1982-83, the percentage of ever-married American Catholics who had ever been divorced or legally separated rose from about 13 percent to about 25 percent. While the proportion of Catholics who have ever been divorced or legally separated is still lower than the proportion in the general population, Catholics have been closing the gap. If the 25 percent is extrapolated to the Catholic population, it means that of the 29 million Catholic adults in the U.S. in 1983 who had ever been married, more than 7 million had been divorced or legally separated at one time.

Second, fragmentary evidence regarding the attitudes and behavior of Catholic youth points to a massive failure by Catholic families to transmit the values of the faith. Sexuality is one dimension of the failure for which some figures are available. The percentage of American Catholics in their 20's who are weekly communicants and who indicated that they think premarital sex is wrong declined from 83 percent in 1963 to 34 percent in 1979. A 1983 study by the Search Institute of Minneapolis that overrepresented children of highly educated, white, midwestern families -- found that 28 percent of the ninth-grade boys and 13 percent of the ninth-grade girls had engaged in sexual intercourse. Analysis of the study according to the church affiliation reveals that the rate of sexual activity among the Catholic young people is higher than among the Protestants.

Why say such things here? Does it not induce gloom to probe the crisis of Catholic family life? Isn't it better to celebrate the flourishing of the good, serious, Catholic families that all of us know?

But surely that is the ostrich-like approach that all of us in this fellowship decry when it is applied to the crisis of teaching in the Church. We here are all convinced that the teaching crisis won't go away unless we confront it. Neither will the pastoral crisis of the family -- although there are many in the church who might like to believe so. It is easy to understand the ostriches. Taking one's head out of the sand means having to face the painful imperative of nonconformity. My challenge is this: let the Fellowship of Catholic Scholars be at the forefront not only of defending Catholic teaching on family life, but also of declaring fearlessly that there is a severe crisis in Catholic family life, for the solutions of which we must seek the help and wisdom of God.

This leads to a second reason for adverting here to the collapse of Catholic family life. It is a subject that calls out for examination by Catholic scholars, especially those in the social sciences. While Madison Avenue spends vast sums on market research, the investment of resources in the careful study of the Catholic family crisis is slight indeed. At its convention next year the Fellowship plans to examine the condition of the American Catholic Church at the dawn of the next century. It is to be hoped that in this way and in others the Fellowship will begin to stimulate honest and helpful study of the breakdown of Catholic family life and of the cultural forces that are contributing to it.

Kevin Perrott
September 1986
F.C.S. Convention, NYC

The Holy and the Good
Relationship Between Religion and Morality in the Thought of Rudolf Otto and Josef Pieper
by
John M. Haas

Few things have appeared more pronounced in the Catholic Church in recent years than the process of desacralization, and nowhere has this process been more relentless than in the United States and Western Europe. Priestly garb and religious habits have almost disappeared. Sanctuaries have been replaced with eucharistic assembly halls. The awesomely enshrined reserved sacrament, the "living heart of our churches" in the words of Paul VI, has often been removed from the sight of the people.

Accompanying the changes in the religious manifestations of our faith have been radically profound ones in the moral sphere as well. Catholics at one time recoiled at the very though of contraception. Abortion was described as unspeakable and abhorrent, as the people of God drew back from the practice with as much dread as they would from the profaning of a sacred and holy object. Homosexual acts elicited a horror more associated with the violation of religious taboos than with simple moral disapproval. But the moral "reformers" have kept pace with their liturgical comrades in the process of desacralization, and today a Catholic moralist can be found discovering ways to excuse anything from racial bigotry to beastiality.[1a] In a word, actions which were once considered unthinkable, such as divorcing and remarrying or renouncing one's vows of celibacy, have lost their startling quality and have become almost commonplace. In light of these parallel developments in the religious and moral spheres, the question might be raised whether some kind of correlation exists between them.

Probably one of the most radical expressions of the secularization process in both religion and morality, again suggesting a link between the two, is found in a book by Timothy E. O'Connell entitled *Principles for a Catholic Morality*. In this book on morality O'Connell writes of religion stating that "quite literally... salvation is a *human* event."[2] "Christians do not really have 'sacred space' in the theological sense... We have gathering places for the community Church, nothing more."[3]

The desacralization of religion so evident in the preceding passages is also expressed in O'Connell's secularist ethic.[4] "Christian ethics, like all of the Christian faith," he writes, "is essentially and profoundly human. It is a human task seeking human wisdom about the human conduct of human affairs.. Thus, in a certain sense, moral theology is not theology at all. It is moral philosophy pursued by people who are believers."[5]

O'Connell's secular Gospel has no room for the sacred in the lives of persons and so offers an ethic which is not burdened by divine precepts. The "fundamental ethical command imposed on the Christian is... 'Be human.' "[6] The Ten Commandments are a "a cultic text with some minimal ethical components,"[7] and, as has been indicated, cult belongs to another age and another mentality.

What is interesting to note in O'Connell's book is the fact that the shift away from an emphasis on the sacred is accompanied by a shift away from certain Catholic moral teachings which have always been considered exceptionless and unchanging, such as the prohibition against the direct killing of innocent human life. Consequently, the question is inevitably raised whether there is some kind of intrinsic relationship between religion and morality, between the holy and the good. This paper can be no more than an initial and limited inquiry into this complex and intriguing question. To address the question, two authors will be discussed who have written of both the moral and the sacred: Rudolf Otto, a German phenomenologist of religion, and the German Thomistic philosopher Josef Pieper. Each man address-ed this question from within his own tradition and consequently makes his own unique contribution to its resolution. Otto was a Lutheran and, philosophically, an idealist. Pieper was a Catholic and, philosophically, a moderate realist. This paper is an inquiry into the way in which these two thinkers developed the relationship between the sacred and the good, and their conviction that an openness to both religion and morality is necessary for the fullest flowering of our humanity.

Rudolf Otto

Rudolf Otto was born in 1869 and died in 1937. He was professor of systematic theology at Marburg who, as a devout Lutheran, looked to the 16th century leader of the Protestant revolt for inspiration in the development of his theories on religious experience.

Otto was strongly influenced by the critical philosophy of Immanuel Kant. Religion for Kant was subordinated to and postulated from morality, a position Otto came to reject. God, freedom and immortality all had to be posited by the mind and could not be directly known, according to Kant. Religion, therefore, came to be removed from the realm of knowledge -- or perhaps the converse could also be said, reason was banished from the realm of religion. The separation of faith & reason was a tendency in the Protestant religion ever since Luther in his reaction to scholasticism showed his deep distrust of reason in the religious sphere by referring to it as "the Devil's whore." Inner subjective experience rather than discursive thought came to be considered as more dependable in the religious spherre in the Lutheran tradition. This is certainly reflected in Otto's thought.

Otto also fell under the influence of the Romantic theologian Friedrich Schleiermacher who taught the centrality of religious experience in order to make religion more accessible to "its cultured despisers." In fact, feeling rather than reason provided for the Romanticist the more dependable grasp of reality.

The task of theology, then, as Otto saw it, was to provide a psychological understanding of concrete experience rather than to provide a dogmatic or systematic exposition of Christian beliefs.

The Idea of the Holy

Otto is best known for his book, *The Idea of the Holy, an Inquiry into the Non-Rational Factor in the Idea of the Divine and its Relation to the Rational*, in which he atttempts to articulate the autonomy and uniqueness of religious experience as distinct from both reason and morality. He wants to free religion from dependence on reason and rationalistic metaphysics which seemed to occur within both scholasticism and Kantianism, even if for different reasons. But, in so doing, his intentions are not antirational. As he says himself, "It will be the task for contemporary Christian teaching... to deepen the rational meaning of the Christian conception of God by permeating it with non-rational elements."[8]

In discussing the unique, autonomous experience of the Holy, Otto analyzed it into its various components, showing that it has more primitive and more developed elements. For the most basic, non-rational element in the experience of the Holy, Otto coined the term "numinous." On the subjective side of this numinous experience is "creature-feeling" or the overwhelming sense of one's nothingness in the face of the absolute power of the Holy. The objective side of the numinous feeling is the experience of a "mysterium" which is both "tremendum" or awe-inspiring and "fascinans" or attractive and delightful. Yet the "mysterium" itself remains unknown and profoundly mysterious. He writes: "The truly 'mysterious' object is beyond our apprehension and comprehension, not only because our knowledge has certain irremovable limits, but because in it we come upon something 'wholly other,' whose kind and character are incommensurable with our own, and before which we therefore recoil in a wonder that strikes us chill and numb."[9]

The numinous constitutes the most primitive, undeveloped sense of the Holy. The numinous "stands for 'the holy' minus its moral factor and... minus its 'rational' aspect altogether."[10] The Holy is not recognized as absolute goodness until the notion has reached the highest stage of its development.

Initially the religious person comes to experience the numinous, not as something good and moral, but simply as a "mysterium tremendum," as something mysterious and peculiarly dreadful. In the face of the "mysterium tremendum," the religious person comes to experience the fear of God which seizes man as something more menacing and overpowering than any created reality. The numinous experience also perceives the "mysterium" which confronts it as "fascinans," i.e., as profoundly attractive and fascinating. This side of the holy comes to be expressed in the divine attributes of love, mercy, pity and compassion. In a sense, these attributes, like the Wrath of God, are seen to be non-rational in that man receives their benefits without meriting them. They are seen as gratuitous and are expressed in such Christian doctrines as the predestination of the elect.

Still, however, the experience of the holy is non-moral. When Otto discusses the holy as a category of value, he points to the experience of two profoundly religious men. When Isaiah is overwhelmed by God's presence in the Temple, he exclaims, "I am a man of unclean lips and dwell among a people of unclean lips." When Peter witnesses God's power in Christ's miraculous deeds, he cries out, "Depart from me, O Lord, for I am a sinful man," However, Otto tells us that we should not regard these exclamations as expressions of moral unworthiness. He writes: "These outbursts of feeling are not simply, and probably not al all, *moral* depreciations, but belong to a quite special category of valuation and appeasement."[11]

These exclamations of depreciation are expressive of the feeling of absolute profaneness in the face of the holy. The feeling is one of profaneness, not immorality, for " 'qadosh' or 'sanctus' is not originally a *moral* category at all."[12]

The Connection Between the Holy and the Good

Once Otto has firmly maintained that the holy is an autonomous, unique, a priori category of experience, independent of reason and morality, he proceeds to argue that reason, morality and the sense of the holy are all intrinsically linked.

Although the numinous is the expression of the holy minus its moral quality, a process of moralization and rationalization occurs to bring the holy to its full development. For example, the experience of the Wrath of God eventually comes to be filled with elements derived for the moral reason: it comes to express God's righteousness punishing moral transgression. One of the primitive non-moral expressions of numinous consciousness in the Old Testament is "daemonic dread" which is illustrated by *Ex.:* 4:24, where God meets Moses by the way and tries to kill him. However, the experience of the numinous does not remain at that level. Otto writes:

> The venerable religion of Moses marks the beginning of a process... by which the numinous is throughout rationalized and moralized, i.e., charged with ethical import, until it becomes the 'holy' in the fullest sense of the word... This moralizing and rationalizing process does not mean that the numinous itself has been overcome, but merely that its preponderance has been overcome. The numinous is at once the basis upon which and the setting within which the ethical and rational meaning is consummated.[13]

The culmination of this moralizing process in the Old Testament is found in the Prophets. But it is in the Gospels that one encounters the "consummation of that process tending to rationalize, moralize, and humanize the idea of God."[14]

Although the moral dimension of holiness reaches its apogee in Jesus, he is not seen merely as a moral teacher. Jesus shows that the "Holy One of Israel" is a "heavenly Father" without losing sight of his holiness. Jesus begins his model prayer with "Our Father... holy be your Name." In fact, everyone associated with Jesus comes to share in the numinosity of God. His followers become known the "holy ones." This title does not mean that the people are morally perfect, as any reading of Paul's letters will show, but that they are "the people who participate in the mystery of the final day."[15]

Although Otto constantly insists on the relationship between reason, morality and numinous experience in the fully developed idea of the Holy, he does not demonstrate it. He says it is merely "*felt* as something axiomatic, something whose inner necessity we feel to be self-evident."[16] Consequently, we can see that his final appeal is made to feeling as a cognitive function, and it seems to be here that Otto's analysis fails. Feeling is not cognitive, but rather arises with cognition. Joy, fear, numinous consciousness arise in response to the cognitive grasp of an object. We must know, possess through knowledge, a desirable object to experience joy. We must know a threatening object (through memory or present knowledge) to experience fear. And the feeling of numinosity would arise only as we were confronted by the holy. There must be an object, a reality, which can be known through the intellect in order to elicit emotion. But, in his idealism, Otto is incapable of moving beyond an analysis of the psychological state of the subject. The "mysterium tremendum," for example, is not something encountered, eliciting dread in the subject, but rather is an expression of a peculiar state of mind in the subject:

> The rational ideas of absoluteness, completion, necessity and substantiality, and no less so those of the good as an objective value, objectively binding and valid, are not to be 'evolved' from any sense of sense-perception. ...Rather, seeking to account for the ideas in question, we are referred away from all sense-experience back to the original and underivable capacity of the mind implanted in the 'pure reason' independently of all perception.[17]

Concluding Remarks

Otto's idealist convictions seem to be the principal obstacle to his articulating a link between the numinous and the moral. The most he is able to do is to insist that we *feel* an inner, necessary interpenetration of the two which includes all the complexity of non-rational experiences. The difficulty is insurmountable since we are unable to get outside the self to the object which elicits the feelings of dread, awe, love and fascination. It is ultimately impossible to know the all-powerful and the all-good. We are left only with the feelings which arise from the encounter.

However, Otto's phenomenological study of religious experience is so perceptive that he cannot help but speak of the holy as well as the experience of it. The common use of language, his objective scholarship and common sense all seem to conspire to lead him beyond a mere analysis of the psychological state to the reality which gives rise to it. He writes, "The numinous is thus felt as objective and outside the self."[18] He frequently speaks of being confronted by the numinous or the holy. In fact, he says that religious feeling "in itself has immediate and primary reference to an object outside the self... This is so manifestly borne out by experience that it must be about the first thing to force itself upon the notice of psychologists analyzing the facts of religion."[19]

Otto may take notice of the awareness of an object outside the subject, but he never investigates it. Consequently, he never identifies the link between the holy and the good.

Josef Pieper

Josef Pieper, born in 1904, was for many years a professor of philosophy at the University of Munsters. Although a philosopher, he frequently addressed religious questions with the Thomistic tradition.

Pieper gave considerable attention to analyses of the sacred,[20] often with insights as penetrating as those of Otto. It was Pieper's conviction that rational reflection on the nature of the human person will reveal dimensions to his personality which not only appear non-rational, in Otto's terminology, but which, as such, help to provide the very basis for a sound rationality open to all of human experience. He writes:

> It is completely natural and human for man not always and exclusively to be practical, to be purposeful -- but occasionally to make a *sign* -- be it only to light a candle *not* to illuminate a room but to give expression to the festive significance of the moment... It is the deliberate *uselessness* of all this that is important, the element of super-abundance and exuberance, of non-calculation and even of waste. The first portion of wine is not used, it is not

drunk, it is squandered, it is shed into the sea or on the floor as a libation in honor of the gods. In the same way Christendom did *not* build practical meeting rooms, but cathedrals...[21]

Pieper argues that there is a sacred reality which transcends reason and upon which reason is grounded. Without this grounding, human reason is left without restraints and begins to assume the posture of the divine, supposing that it can determine and create reality rather than discover it. The sense of the sacred with its non-rational ground becomes lost and even the most sacred realtiy known to us, the individual human life, becomes merely a usable and disposable means toward attaining whatever end a man chooses for himself.

One of the greatest intellects the western world ever produced, Thomas Aquinas, never forgot the limited role of reason even though he utilized it as few ever had. Thomas was able to make proper use of reason, according to Pieper, because he had an abiding awareness of the sacred underlying all those things which were open to his senses and his intellect. Although known for the dispassionate use of his reason, his spiritual sensitivity is evidenced in the beautiful hymns he wrote for the Feast of Corpus Christi. Also a celebrated experience which occurred later in his life is witness to his openness to the holy. In Pieper's book *The Silence of St. Thomas* he writes of a profoundly mystical experience which occured in Thomas' life in 1273 on the Feast of St. Nicholas and which resulted in the end of his writing career. Returning to work after Mass, Thomas encountered an overwhelming experience of he superabundance and power of God's presence. He was so stunned by the experience he put aside the treatise on the Sacrament of Penance he had been writing for the *Summa Theologica* and never wrote again. When Thomas' friend and companion, Reginald of Piperno, asked what had come over him, Thomas could only reply, "I can write no more. All that I have written seems to me nothing but straw... compared to what I have seen and what has been revealed to me."[22]

There is in the writings as well as the life of Thomas ample evidence of what *Otto* calls the non-rational, numinous element in religious experience. God, for Thomas, remains forever hidden, ultimately unknown to the human mind. Because of His utter transcendence, the "otherness" to which Otto refers, God is never reducible to any of our rational categories or mental concepts. Thomas acknowledges this fact when he writes, "Because we are not capable of knowing what God is but only what He is not, we cannot contemplate how God is but only how He is not."[23] And in the "Questio Disputata de Potentia Dei" he writes, "This is the ultimate in human knowledge of God: to know that we do not know Him."[24]

The fact that we cannot ultimately know God should always be kept in mind when we engage in theological reflection in order to avoid the constant temptation to reduce God to rational concepts. However, the fact that we cannot know God as He is in Himself does not mean that we cannot know anything about Him. As Thomas tells us, "Although we cannot know the essence of God, nevertheless in (theology) we make use of his effects."[25] Indeed, all we can come to know naturally of God, we know through our experience of the world of sense around us.

It is here that a major difference develops between the idealist approach of Otto and the realist approach followed by Pieper. It will be remembered that Otto insisted that the religious ideas he discussed by "referred away from all sense-experience back to an original and underivable capacity of the mind implanted in the 'pure reason' independently of all perception." Yet Thomas, and following him, Pieper, will come to base all arguments for the existence of God on observable, empirical data and show that a sound contemplation of them will lead one to understand that God exists. Thomas does not recoil from the data of sense experience, but views that as effects of something and in a sense goes *through* them to some understanding of their ultimate cause. In other words, it is only through the senses, through our encounter with the objective world of reality, that we can come to know something of God, however limited that knowledge is.

For all the religious and psychological factors which contributed to the Jewish reluctance to utter the Divine Name, that reluctance did give testimony to a rational truth: God cannot be directly known. Even the most proper name for God, HE WHO IS, cannot capture His essence. So the Jew remains silent. This fact was recognized by Thomas as well:

> ... the existence of God in His essence itself.... Now our intellect cannot know the essence of God itself in this life, as it is in itself, but whatever mode it applies in determining what it understands about God, it falls short of the mode of what God is in Himself. Therefore the less determinate the names are, and the more universal and absolute they are, the more properly they applied to God... Therefore HE WHO IS is the most proper Name of God.[26]

It is only by knowing the limitations of our reason that we can presume to say anything of God. We must always realize that what we do say of Him can be understood only in an analogical not a univocal sense. None of this is to deny the object of our religious experience, but only to say that it is unfathomable. As Pieper points out, "The more intensely we pursue (the) ways of knowledge, the more is revealed to us -- of the *darkness*, but also of the *reality* of the mystery."[27] Indeed, the *only* avenue open to that ineffable mystery are the objects of its creative and sustaining power which are held up to our senses, which can be known through sense experience.

As it has been pointed out, Thomas looks to the effects of God's creative power to know something of God. And it is through an awareness of their being that Being Itself can be known of. Mysticism, therefore, does not mean a turning *away from* the world of sense, but rather a turning toward it. The sacred is always mediated through a physical reality, a tree, a mountain, a hillside, the sound of music, the words of the prophet, the stillness of nature. Through his attention to realtiy Thomas was always aware of the sacral character of Being. Perhaps it would not be too unscholarly to suggest that Thomas's experience of 1273 was an experience of self-subsisting Being, pure act, whose essence is existence, the source and Creator of all that is.

The Connection Between the Holy and the Good

At this point, attention should be turned to the objects of man's experience to see if the connection between the holy and the good may be grounded in reality itself.

It must be remembered that the only being whose existence is necessary is God. Pieper writes: "It is impossible that the substance of any being other than the First Agent be its very act-of-being... It belongs to (God) alone that His substance is nothing other than His act-of-being."[28] As Etienne Gilson points out, reminiscent of Otto, "WHO IS signified: He whose essence is to exist; WHO IS is the proper name of God; consequently, the essence of anything that is not God is not to exist."[29]

Everything, therefore, which can be encountered through the senses must be understood as "creatura." God is the Creator, all else is creature, and utterly dependent on Him.

Pieper maintains that this notion of creation, of all things being essentially dependent on God, is the key to a correct understanding of Thomistic philosophy. The notion of creation, says Pieper, determines and characterizes the interior structure of *nearly all* the basic concepts in St. Thomas's philosophy of Being.

A basic scholastic maxim, "ens et verum et bonum convertuntur," is essential to the thesis that the link between the holy and the good can be found in reality. Pieper insists that propositions such as "all that exists is good" or "all that exists is true" cannot be understood "...unless it be realized that the concepts and theses in question do not refer to a neutral Being that simply exists, not to an 'ens ut sic,' not to an indeterminate world of 'objects,' but formally to Being as creatura."[30]

Pieper accepts to a degree the proposition common in western thought that "truth" cannot be predicated of what really exists but only of what is thought. He still wants to be able to speak of knowing the truth of reality. Pieper does this by demonstrating that, in the Christian understanding of creation, things exist by virtue of their being products of the creative thought of God's mind. He writes: "The essence of things is that they are creatively thought."[31] Human artifacts, for example, have specific natures because they have been determined by the creative mind. For example, one can speak of the "nature" of a pen because the constructive intellect has invented a pen. Sartre insisted on this insight, saying that there is no nature in things which have not been manufactured. Consequently, he said, it would be impossible to have a human nature since there exists no God to think it creatively.

According to Pieper, however, it is precisely because the world has been creatively thought by God that we can speak of the nature and the truth of things. The real world is able to be known by men because it stands between two knowing intellects. As St. Thomas puts it: "Res naturalis inter duos intellectus constituta est."[32] The two subjects are, of course, the divine intellect and the human intellect. The creative knowledge of God gives measure to reality but receives none ("mensurans non mensuratum"). Created reality is at once measured by God's knowledge and itself gives measure to the human mind. It possesses intrinsic knowability for the mind ("mensuratum et mensurans"). Finally there is human knowledge which is given measure by reality but itself does not give measure, except to artifacts and acts ("mensuratum non mensurans"). The reality of things consists in their being creatively thought by the Creator. Things, as "creaturae," correspond to the archetype of them in the creative mind of God. These things are true for man in so far as his mind "receives its measure" from them, corresponding to their objective reality. Pieper writes: " 'True'... is an ontological name, a synonym for 'real.' 'Ens et verum convertuntur.' "[33] Because God gives measure to and bestows essence on things through his creative intellect, they are able to be known by the human intellect. However, even created things cannot be completely fathomed. As Thomas says, "The essential grounds of things are unknown to us."[34] Things cannot be known in their essence as the essence is related to God. Consequently, "We do not know substantial forms as they are in themselves."[35] Pieper also quotes Thomas to the effect that "essential differences are unknown to us,"[36] and "created things are darkness in so far as they proceed from nothing."[37]

Even the objects of our sense experience have a mysterious dimension or quality to them. Not only God in His perfect Being has an unutterable Name, but so do the things which are encountered in the world. Indeed, through their essential relation as creatures to the Creator, created things not only are unfathomable in themselves but also serve as the means for mediating an awareness of the reality of the totally transcendent and all-powerful Creator to men. It is precisely in the objects of sense experience, then, that the holy is encountered and arouses in the religiously sensitive soul such overwhelming feelings of dread, awe and fascination. Something of the numinous, of the "mysterium tremendum et fascinans," is encountered in the objects of reality.

If we locate the object which gives rise to the numinous consciousness in created reality (without, of course, being so foolish as to try to "capture" the holy there), how do we establish the necessary link between numinous consciousness and the sense of morality? Otto never demonstrated the conjunction of the holy and the good, but simply insisted that it invariably occurs.[38] Pieper, on the other hand, argued that morality arises from the encounter with objective reality, the same source whence arise the awareness of the sacred and feelings of religious awe.

As has been said, things through their essence express God only in an imperfect manner since things are creatures and the created cannot wholly express the Creator. But they *do* express God for us, even if imperfectly, and are to be viewed as good, for insofar as they exist they do so in relation to their creative source who is God. It has also been said that their essence cannot be known in their relation to God. Yet even though the essence of things cannot be completely grasped, it is not unknowable. As Pieper says: "Man's intellectual power enables him to penetrate to the essence of things; there can be, therefore, insights and assertions concerning the nature of things which, though not exhaustive, are nevertheless true."[39]

How is it that things can be both inscrutable and knowable to the human intellect? The answer lies, according to Pieper, in the notion of "creatura" which pervades the philosophy of Thomas. It is because things are created, because they come forth from the archetype in the creative intellect of God, that they can be known and, at the same time, remain unfathomable. Because they are rooted in the divine Logos, they partake of His lucid rationality. They can, therefore, be known to the human intellect. But in that they issue forth from the divine, they cannot be known in the ground of their being.

Moreover, in so far as anything exists, it is known as good. "To be good is really the same thing as to exist," Thomas tells us.[40] Being and the true as convertible terms are also convertible with the good. The aspect of self-subsisting Being understood as good would correspond to the "mysterium fascinans" of Otto's analysis. It is perceived as appealing, as delectable, as desirable. Indeed everything which exists, which participates in being through the creative act of self-subsisting Being, is good.

The good serves as the motivation for human acts. All things seek the good, seek their full realization, by acting. The human agent acts consciously on behalf of the good understood as the end or "terminus" of his action as well as its motivation. Thomas writes: "Every agent acts for an end, since all things seek the good. Now for the agent's action to be suited to the end, it must be adapted and proportionate to it, and this cannot be done save by an intellect that is cognizant both of the end and of its nature as end and again of the proportion between the end and the means..."[41]

As one commentator on Aquinas writes, "All human life both in ourselves and in others consists in a search for (objective, ontological) goods outside and beyond ourselves which have been grasped by our minds and accepted by our free wills as worthy of our search."[42] All of our actions are on behalf of ends perceived as good. This is metaphysical principle which is obvious upon reflection. The principle is as necessary to explain free, rational action as the principle of contradiction is necessary to explain rational thought.

For the agent to act, his intellect must grasp the end on behalf of which he would act and present it to the will as something desirable. It is the speculative intellect which first grasps simple reality. By knowing reality it comes to know that on behalf of which it would act and in a sense expresses itself *as the practical intellect* when it considers that which is to be done. Pieper is strong in insisting on the unity of the practical and speculative intellects saying that the "concept of the practical reason necessarily includes and asserts the theoretical reason as well. The 'basic faculty' is the theoretical reason, which 'extends' to become the practical.[43] The practical reason, according to Pieper, is nothing but the theoretical reason regarded under the special function of directing action.

There is, of course, only one faculty of intellect in man. Its task, in terms of human action, is to see that persons act in accord with objective reality, itself understood as the good which it is. In terms of what has already been said, objective reality can be known in its essence although not fully comprehended. This objective reality not only presents itself as numinous under the aspect of religion, but also as good and worthy of acting on behalf of under the aspect of morality. A realist epistemology can lead to an intellectualist ethic which can develop into an ethical realism grounded in the objective order of reality.

Not only are material goods encountered and sought through objective reality, such as offspring, a home, adequate wealth, but so are spiritual goods. Love and justice are goods of reality on behalf of which we act. Even these spiritual goods arise from the proper ordering and relationships of the material goods which we encounter. Such realities give measure ("mensurans") to the mind which conforms to and in a sense becomes essentially those realities. Pieper writes: "Knowledge of the nature of the good necessarily includes the previous awareness of the essential structure of reality as such."[44]

Yet once the mind receives measure from created reality, it seeks its greater realization and gives measure or form to the act which it proposes. The agent is free to act on behalf of the good, and the essence of the morally good act is that the agent knowingly and freely acts on behalf of the good. The real always seeks to become more fully that which it is, and therein lies its goodness. Again, to quote Pieper: "The good is nothing else than this goal and end of the movement of being, the realization of the essence. 'Everything has as much of goodness as it has of being.' Perfection and the good mean nothing else than the 'plenitude of being,' 'plenitudo essendi.' "[45]

It would seem that the sense of both morality and the holy arise from the same source: created reality in relation to its uncreated ground. Morality seeks the "plenitudo essendi" through action and the dread experience of the holy results whenever this "plenitudo essendi" is encountered in its depths. If morality consists in freely acting on behalf of true goods known through a sure grasp of reality, the sense of the holy consists in an awareness of the essential depths of the same reality.

Conclusion

Are the holy and the good necessarily linked? They are in so far as they both arise from the same source, created reality in relation to its uncreated ground. Yet there can be good men who have never had an experience of the holy, and there have been religious men who have not been very moral. King David's awareness of God's transcendent majesty did not prevent him from committing adultery. And certain religions with a keen sense of the numinous have a poorly developed sense of morality. Otto places Islam in this category.

There are contemporary examples of religious awareness coupled with moral underdevelopment. A book by Daniel Maguire deals with morality and includes many beautiful passages extolling the affective beauty and importance of religious experience for the moral life. He argues that moral action is "traceable to what could be called a mystical perception of the inviolable sanctity of human life... This mystical perception undergirds every moral ought and those who are alien to it are alien to moral consciousness."[46] Yet in the book Maguire argues for abortion, suicide and homosexual liaisons. For some reason, the "mystical perception" Maguire speaks of was incapable of saving him from significant error in the moral sphere. It might be argued that his religious experience was a counterfeit one, but that would be possibly an unjust accusation and certainly one which could not be substantiated. It can be argued, however, that his moral methodology is inadequate. He is basically an intuitionist, unable to ground his ethics either in the agent or in the objective order of reality. What does him a disservice is not his religious experience, but a philosophy inadequate to the task.

When a realist senses the inviolable sacredness of a human life, he soundly draws the conclusion that it may never under any circumstances be directly violated. He grasps its intrinsic goodness and knows that he may only act on its behalf. To violate it, to act against it, would do violence to what he knows it to be, a good on behalf of which he may or may not act. To act directly against it would be to view it as an evil to be eliminated in order to attain something else viewed as a good, since one always acts on behalf of a good. The reason a Catholic justly recoils from acts of contraception, homosexuality, racism, suicide or abortion is because he is horrified at the sight of an inviolable and sacred good being violated within those acts.

There is clearly a link between religion and morality, but, in order for it to bear the richest fruit, the religion must be the true one and the morality must be guided by a sound epistemology. The Catholic Church has been divinely guaranteed infallibility in the teaching of religious and moral truth. Two of the greatest aids to her in this task have been as follows: (1) a sacramental liturgical and devotional life capable of arousing the most profound religious experiences and of being the source of the objective assistance of divine grace, and (2) a providentially provided realist epistemology enabling it to show correctly, though inadequately, how we can know the truth which will set us free. The sense of religious awe prevents reason from puffing itself up to idolatrous dimensions, and the realist epistemology prevents the religious experience from degenerating into subjective intuitionism, especially in the area of morality.

Man is not only a rational animal but also a religious one. To deny either of these aspects of his personhood is to make him less than he ought to be. Some people have very limited intellectual capabilities; others a stunted religious sense. But a full flowering of all human potentialities simply makes us more human. One of the tragic concomitants to the growing secularism in the Church is the denial to many in our contemporary society of the opportunity to become fully human. O'Connell upheld the truth when he said the highest moral demand placed on Christians was to be fully human. Unfortunately, his insistence on desacralization evidenced a false anthropology, a lack of understanding of what it means to be fully human. As Pieper points out, "...the teaching and practice of the Church -- which from earliest times has persistently maintained the rites of the sacred -- are in correpsondence with the reality of man... The advocates of desacralization began by denying nature -- by denying man's orientation to the sacred."[47]

Conclusion

I believe it has been shown that morality and religion are essentially, i.e., ontologically, linked whether or not both play an equally significant role in any one person's life. I also believe that each can suffer without the influence of the other.

Morality without the influence of religion faces the danger of degenerating to a utilitarian rationalism. With no cognizance of the realm of the sacred there is the danger that the world will lose its sense of awe and mystery. Reality will come to be viewed as totally comprehensible and, therefore, totally manageable. Nothing will any longer excite wonder, provoke humility, demand respect. Pieper writes:

> The danger inherent in this situation is that man might, erroneously, come to regard the world as a whole and the created things with it -- above all, man himself -- in the same manner in which he regards, correctly, his own artifacts... In other words, man is beginning to consider the whole of creation as completely fathomable, fully accessible to rational comprehension, and, above all, as something which it is permissible to change, transform or even destroy.[48]

The twentieth century has, of course, witnessed the death of God and the desacralization of the world. With the elimination of the sacred there disappeared the sense of dread and of wonder and love before anything or anyone. The world became malleable, and made over in man's own image. Human life became expendable and totalitarian states came to use it as the raw material for their own designs. Without the clear demarcation of sacred and profane, limits and structures and boundaries dissolved and social and private lives descended into chaos. No longer chastened by the overwhelming power of the holy, reason enthroned itself as divine. No longer placing itself at the service of man, reason subordinated man to its own ends, unrestricted, or, so it thought, by the limits imposed by a divinely created nature and its enduring order.

To lead her people out of the current wilderness, the Church must stringently apply a disciplined reason to the mysteries of life and faith, as well as maintain a profound sense of how unfathomable and inexhaustible those mysteries are. It was this juxtaposition of traits in the Catholic Church which Otto could not understand and yet which had traditionally redounded to her glory. Through a rigorous use of reason and a sensitive use of evocative symbols and liturgical gestures, the Church can still call forth from persons the full realizations of their potential to be fully human. To enable persons to be fully morally responsive, the Church must guard with care the sacred rites which have been entrusted to her.

It is true that the fear of the Lord is only the beginning of wisdom. Similarly, the awareness of the sacred may be only the beginning of morality. But it is an important beginning and a lasting component. Perhaps nothing could be more important for instilling the beginning of moral wisdom in the people of God than for the priest, through his gestures and attire and bearing, to elicit in the people a sense of stupor and wonder, of awe and admiration, of dread and exaltation in the face of the ineffable presence of God Himself upon the altar and tabernacle, the consecrated spaces of the Catholic Church.

1a. Cf. Timothy E. O'Connell, *Principles for a Catholic Morality* (New York: The Seabury Press, 1978) and Anthony Kosnik, et al., *Human Sexuality* (New York: Paulist Press, 1978).

2. Timothy E. O'Connell, *Principles for a Catholic Moraltiy* (New York: The Seabury Press, 1978), p. 38

3. *Ibid.,* p. 39.

4. *Ibid.,* p. 39.

5. *Ibid.,* p. 40.

6. *Ibid.,* p. 39.

7. *Ibid.,* p. 129.

8. Rudolf Otto, *The Idea of the Holy* (New York: Oxford University Press, 1957), p. 108.

9. *Ibid.,* p. 28.

10. *Ibid.,* p. 6.

11. Otto, *Holy,* p. 51.

12. *Ibid.,* p. 52.

13. Otto, *Holy* p. 75.

14. *Ibid.,* p. 82.

15. *Ibid.,* p. 84.

16. *Ibid.,* p. 140.

17. *Ibid.,* p. 112.

18. *Ibid.,* p. 11.

19. *Ibid.,* p. 10.

20. Some of his writings which concern this theme are *In Tune With the World*; *Leisure, the Basis of Culture*; *The Silence of St. Thomas*; *The Realm of the Sacred*.

21. Josef Pieper, "The Realm of the Sacred", *Triumph*, November, 1971, p. 22.

22. Josef Pieper, *The Silence of St. Thomas* (New York: Pantheon, 1957), p. 39-40.

23. S.T., 1a, 3, prologue.

24. Pot.Dei, 7, 5, ad 14.

25. S.T., 1a, 1, 7.

26. S.T., 1a, 13, 11.

27. Pieper, *Silence*, p. 38.

28. C.G., II, 52.

29. Etienne Gilson, *The Christian Philosophy of St. Thomas Aquinas* (New York: Random House, 1956), p. 93.

November, 1971, p. 22

30. Pieper, *Silence*, p. 48.

31. *Ibid.*,, p. 51.

32. Questiones Disputatae de Veritate, 1, 2.

33. Pieper, *Silence*, p. 58.

34. de Anima, I, 1, 15.

35. Questione Disputata de Spiritualibus Creaturis, II ad 3.

36. de Veritate, 4, I ad 8.

37. de Veritate, 18, 2 ad 5. Cf., also Gilson, *Christian Philosophy*, pp. 221-2.

38. It is interesting to note that Otto argues that Christianity is the highest religion because it most successfully and completely rationalizes and moralizes the numinous. Islam, a lower religion in Otto's judgement, has not moralized the numinous as effectively as Christianity and is victim to the more irrational elements of the numinous.

39. Pieper, *Silence*, p. 95.

40. S.T., 1a, 5, 1.

41. Pot. Dei, 1, 5.

42. Augustine Joseph Brennan, *Moral Action in Aristotle and Aquinas* (Sidney: The Cresta Printing Co.), p. 3.

43. Josef Pieper, *Reality and the Good* (Chicago: Henry Regnery Company, 1967), p. 49.

44. *Ibid.,* p. 68.

45. *Ibid.,* p. 69.

46. Daniel Maguire, *The Moral Choice* (Garden City, New York: Doubleday, 1978), p. 81.

47. Pieper, *"Realm of the Secret"*, p. 20.

48. Pieper, *Silence*, p. 92.

Response
by
Joseph Boyle

John Haas begins by noting two phenoamena within the post Vatican II Church: a process of desacralization by which he means a decline in the manifestation of a deep sense of awe and reverence in the face of the transcendent reality of God, and a growing rejection, both in the theory and the practice of Catholics, of the precepts of Christian morality.

His paper is a meditation on the connection between these two phenomena, and an attempt to articulate a reasonable response to them on the part of the Church. He points out that the relationship between religious sensitivity and moral life and thought is a complex one: some, who reject Christian morality, speak movingly of the awareness of God in their lives and, indeed, on their moral views; others justify their rejection of Christian morality by denying the sacral character of Christian life and holding that Christian ethics must be utterly secular.

He explores the connection between religion and morality in the Thomistic manner, by first considering the holy -- the object of religion -- and the good -- the object of morality, and then by inquiring how these objects are related.

Professor Hass makes use of the analysis of Rudolf Otto, according to whom the category of the holy is built up from an elementary concept of the numinous by the addition of rational and moral components. Otto's concept of the numinous is elementary in several ways: it is the most basic element of the concept of the holy and, so it seems, it refers to an irreducible part of human experience. By saying this concept is of a nonrational form of experience, Otto means that the awareness involved in the feeling of the numinous is not propositional. It is not the kind of emotion which might be caused by a believer's affirming in faith the propositions of the Creed. Neither is it prompted by an awareness of something known by inference --nor by a feeling provoked by knowing the conclusion of an arguement for God's existence.

The subjective side of this experience is what Otto calls "creature feeling," i.e., the sense of one's nothingness in the face of the transcendent. The objective side -- that which, within the experience itself provokes this creature feeling -- is Otto's *mysterium tremendum et fascinans* -- an object beyond our comprehension and, at the same time, awe inspiring yet attractive and delightful.

I find all this very mysterious I suppose because I never have had such an experience. My religious *beliefs* provoke strong feelings, but I am aware of no special religious feeling irreducible to normal emotional reactions from beliefs of such a wonderful kind as God has given to those who believe. But John Haas is more irenical towards German metaphysicians than I am capable of being, and he focuses on what is correct in Otto's analysis; a person's awareness of God quite naturally involves awe and fascination in the face of one so great and transcendently mysterious.

Haas's concern is with how Otto manages to connect this kind of experience to morality. For Otto thinks that the fully developed concept of the holy involves moral as well as numinous components. But the connection is by way of feeling: the connection between the numinous and morality is "...felt as something axiomatic, something whose inner necessity we feel to be self-evident." Professor Haas objects that this will not do. According to Otto's analysis, he argues, morality is only accidentally connected with religion.

But I wonder if the connection between Otto's numinous experience and any proposition whatsoever about God or his relation to us would be any less accidental. Is the content of numinous experience or part of it truly expressed by the reality affirmed when one says: I believe in God, the Father Almighty, Creator of Heaven and Earth? If so, the experience of the numinous isn't so nonrational after all. If not, then the relationship is accidental and either the numinous sits in judgement on the Creed or vice versa. If the latter, then the numinous, as conceived by Otto, cannot be central to Christian religion; if the former, there is nothing at all mysterious about the *non*-connection between religion and morality. For if the Creed is not essential to religion, then how much less essential are merely moral propositions.

Professor Haas turns from Otto to a more satisfactory account of the relation between morality and religion in the work of Thomist philosopher Josef Pieper. To put the matter more briefly and with perhaps more interpretation than is fair to Haas, what I take him to be saying is this: Peiper is helpful because of his emphasis on the transcendence of God and the real limitations of the human intellect in knowing God. According to the realistic epistemology assumed and endorsed by the Church, we do not know God directly but through the creatures which are known initially by sense experience. We do not comprehend God. We know that he exists, not what he is. Moreover, in coming to a limited knowledge of God through his creatures, we come to know them as creatures, and this accounts for the sense of wonder and mystery we have even concerning created reality.

Among the things we know about the created world is the true good for human beings. This true good is the basis of morality, and morality is seen in its most proper perspective when seen as part of God's creation. Understood in this way, human lives can be said to be holy. For the fullness of being towards which morality directs us is in its most perfect form the absolutely perfect being of God. In the depths of true morality, we find the holy.

Seeing morality in this way, Haas observes, prevents the exaltation of human reasoning characteristic of modern ethical thinking. For superficial rationalism can arise only if we ignore the depth and mystery of created reality, including our own lives. His prescription follows almost deductively: the Church must strengthen its efforts to nourish in the faithful a lively sense of the mystery and transcendence of God. Much can be done in this area, and relatively easily, if the celebration of the mysteries of the faith is conducted with the care and reverence which their reality and meaning demand.

I would add only one point, which Prof. Haas refers to generically and surely does not deny. The mysteries of our faith celebrated in the Eucharist and the other sacraments have a very direct and definite connection to our moral lives. Indeed, as Germain Grisez has argued, the sacraments are in a way principles of Christian moral life. For in the sacraments we join with the actions of Jesus and his Church. To do this well, we must know what we are doing. And intelligently living the sacramental life of the Church is crucial today. Many Catholics live much of their lives (and perhaps all of us live some of our lives) in pursuit of the "this worldly" happiness promised by modern secularism, even if such lives are enlivened from time to time by numinous experiences. In this framework, Christian morality does not make sense: moral absolutes, for example, might seem noble or abstractly reasonable to someone thinking from this perspective, but to actually live by them, when that causes great pain and personal suffering, is not sensible. Turning one's cheek, laying down one's life, and so on, make even less sense. Christian morality only makes sense for people whose concern is for heaven. And intelligent participation in the sacramental life of the Church makes that goal palpable. For in the sacraments we not only symbolize the saving actions of Our Lord, we join in them.

This requires instruction and expression in the conduct of the sacraments. I think that the changes in the liturgy mandated in the Vatican Council sought to this expression, even though in the judgment of some they have removed some of the majesty and awe from the liturgy. Practical understanding of our sacramental life is, of course, in no way inimical to the sense of the awesome sacredness in which we participate: quite to the contrary.

Joseph Boyle
St. Michaels College
University of Toronto

Spiritual Direction Through
Catholic Education
by
Jude P. Dougherty

To speak of Catholic education is to acknowledge, for one thing, a specific telos to education, and, for another a distinctive tradition. The recognition of that telos is, of course, shared by other believers. It consists of the awareness that the grave is not the end of man, that man is called to a life in union with the divine. Acknowledgment of this transcendent end colors the whole of education. At no stage is ultimate fulfillment confused with terrestrial happiness.

The distinctive feature of Catholic education is the Catholic tradition itself, a very complex tradition spanning two thousand years of history. One need only enter the Basilica of St. Ambrose in Milan to have the historical asserted. There under the high altar lay the remains of Ambrose who died in 397 along with the remains of Saints Gervase and Protase, both first-century martyrs.

Physical continuity is a visible reminder of intellectual inheritance. Ambrose taught Augustine and Augustine taught the West. The Fathers, no less than the Greeks and Romans upon whom they drew, were concerned with education. From Augustine's *De Magistro* to Newman's *Idea of a University*, one can find hundreds of books, some of them Christian and literary classics, which speak to the aims of education. In common they recognize that the end of life is the Beatific Vision and that the road to this vision requires a kind of interiority, even in the midst of the crassest temporal pursuits.

By the interior life, I mean the life of the intellect as it draws upon the experience of the present, interpreted within the context of an appropriated past, in order to be future oriented in a movement whose ultimate end is nothing less than self-fulfillment. Christ himself is the model. He came to proclaim a new law, but in doing so was respectful of the best of ancient codes. He drew upon his listeners' grasp of nature's laws, and, on that foundation, taught those things that unaided intellect alone could not fathom. His disciples found him credible. When St. John Chrysostom sought an empirical proof for the existence of God, he found it in the splendor of the Church. The evidence came from the fact that the Church in its teaching appealed to noble and low, rich and poor, learned and not, and in a brief span had succeeded in transforming the lives of individuals and nations for the better. An institution which produced such good effects, thought Chrysostom, could only have a divine origin.

Three things I wish to underscore: the requirement of critical intelligence, the need for learning, and the need for the Church. Unaided intelligence will not suffice. Isolated from tradition and from community it will become as sterile as Hume's believer, sequestered in a private meditation for a moment in the confines of his study. Just as a knowledge of the practical arts is required for success in most of life's activities, so, too, in matters of religious activity, learning is required. It would be foolish to proceed as if God and the way to God were unknown. Religion is a communal activity. The acknowledgment of God's existence, the acknowledgment of man's debt to Him, and an awareness of the propriety of paying that debt are communal affairs. Awareness of the need to worship is found wherever men are found. Piety is thus a natural virtue. "Spirituality" is but a term for the lifting of intellect and will to things divine. It is a habit of referral, grounded in contemplation; a habit of understanding things in the light of their finality.

The love of God requires some knowledge of God. No one can love an unknown God. God has to be present in some manner before his goodness can command the volitional act. Awareness is the result of some act on our part. It is the result of our attentiveness to a witness, be it oral or written. The normal channel of awareness is parental teaching reinforced by formal education. Formal education can carry us to the heights of theological speculation, but the basic truths which ground appreciation are simple and are available to the whole of mankind. There are degrees of knowledge and there are degrees of appreciation. Natural knowledge is complemented by revelation, and he who hears and is privileged to possess the best of human knowledge can advance without limit. Development is open-ended. Like science, the augmentation of a knowledge of things divine profits from concerted effort. Rational disputation is social. John of the Cross and Teresa of Avila were learned people. They made use of both native intelligence and education to ferret out the secrets of the divine.

However, interior life is not to be confused with a life of introspection. The latter is fraught with danger. Self-questioning, which leads to a constant scrutiny of motives, to a perpetual assessment of goals, can distract one form the proper task. Introspection can generate unhappiness and dissatisfaction. One may object that there can be no progress unless one is dissatisfied with one' self. Did not Socrates proclaim as much? With the interior life, as with all things, there is a knowable objective order to which one must conform if one is to be successful. One need not begin as if human nature first came into being with one's self.

The interior life is the life of the mind in the context of divine revelation buttressed by centuries of ecclesiastical teaching. That life of the mind is object-directed even in the depths of its interiority. It seeks, as Socrates taught, a tripartite wisdom: a knowledge of one's self in the light of self, a knowledge of one's self in the light of nature, and a knowledge of one's self in the light of God. It proceeds with confidence that there is objective knowledge about human nature, about the material order, and about God. To know who one is is to first identify with mankind, while recognizing the vagaries of inheritance, chance, custom and geographic setting. One's possibilities and limitations can only be assessed in context. That context includes nature. Avila is not the Grand Meteora. Other things must be borne in mind: intelligence is not evenly distributed; nor are health, nervous constitutions or other physical traits which influence behavior. Man, while rational, is an animal. The great rule-givers in the history of Western monasticism recognized that and provided accordingly. Only so much can be tolerated by the human body without psychic damage. What is possible and what is not is knowable after centuries of experience and reflection. If one is not to go it alone, one has to appropriate that knowledge through study. Given man's discursive mode of intelligence, study is necessarily protracted. If knowledge of nature is difficult, how much more is a knowledge of God. With respect to nature, human nature, and God, there are sciences with principles, methodologies and laws that demand recognition. Those principles and laws, once acknowledged, begin to control. Where an over-zealousness might otherwise prevail, they mitigate excessive bodily deprivation and prevent flights of fancy in divine meditation. While we may be amused by tales of Don Giovanni arguing with the Crucified Christ about his problems with the Communist mayor, we would not take the fictional priest as an example to be followed in ordering our interior life.

The contemplative mind is a discursive mind. It combines and divides and proceeds from one judgment to another. It feeds off experience: its own and what it knows of the experience of others. When it takes God as its object, it focuses most often upon the person of Christ. The life of Christ is available to all. It supplies an object, a focus of the imagination as well as a fount of learning. His teaching and his person co-mingle into an awesome whole. But Christ has to be understood within the context of a triune God, and creating, begetting, bequeathing God who not only gave us his son but a Church infused with his Spirit. Unaided imagination without the teaching of the Church cannot fully grasp the significance of the man from Galilee. That teaching itself is not ready-made but requires the efforts of the wisest of men, adjudicated by the successors of the apostles. Without the authoritative influence of the Church all too fallible intellect can go astray. Perhaps no one was more aware of this than the great Origen who wrote: "I want to be a man of the Church. I do not want to be called by the name of some founder of a heresy but by the name of Christ, and to bear that name which is blesed on the earth; it is my desire, in deed as in spirit, both to be and to be called a Christian." Origen, who was certainly one of the greatest theologians of his day, a man who inspired Jerome and Ambrose, also had a realistic appreciation of the limited role of the theologian in the Church. "If I," he said, "who seem to be your right hand and am called a presbyter and seem to preach the word of God, if I do something against the discipline of the Church and the rule of the Gospel so that I become a scandal to you, the Church, then may the whole of the Church, in unanimous resolve, cut me, its right hand, off, and throw me away." What makes a theology useful to the believer is that it is grounded in a shared insight. Theologies can be plural. The Church, though it has recommended some, does not adjudicate between theologies; the propositions which they engender, yes. It can say that teaching is consistent with the tradition, or that such teaching is deficient and requires re-examination. The starting point of theology is propositions given on the side of faith. But what one makes of those propositions is determined by the philosophical intelligence one brings to their explication. Theologies differ because philosophies differ. There can be a plurality of roads to the same affirmation; but usually not. If one believes that philosophy is a science, one must believe that theology is a science. From agreed-upon data, whether garnered by faith or reason, the conclusions flow. As long as the discourse is straight, and all parties are talking about the same thing, arguments can be checked for accuracy.

The discursive intelligence of the theologian, sometimes the poet-theologian, grounded as it is in Sacred Scripture and in its knowledge of nature, can lead the contemplative mind along fruitful paths and to the heights of human insight. God's grace and special intervention may produce that infrequent special witness we call the "mystic." Some spiritual writers say all are called to the mystical life; but none say to the same degree. We appreciate to the extent that our natural light and learning permit. The child with all his might can love the Crucified Christ and the intensity of his love may never be surpassed in later life; but the object of that love will grow with the understanding that comes with effort and with maturity. To remain childlike in matters of faith is to retain the intensity of love while expanding its object. The hound of heaven pursues endlessly throughout temporal life. The chase ends only when the pursued has been admitted to the Beatific Vision.

It is sometimes said that the God of the philosophers is not the God of Abraham, Isaac and Jacob, but this remark fails to acknowledge a vast difference between philosophies. Certainly the God of Aquinas is compatible with the God of Revelation. The same could be said for the philosophical God embraced by the Fathers and of that subscribed to by nearly all of the medieval doctors. One may not recognize Whitehead's God or Hartshorne's God in the pages of the Hebrew Bible. It is evident that not all philosophy will be of assistance to the believer as he seeks to know better the object of his quest. God has revealed himself in the Sacred Scriptures but he remains an elusive God nevertheless. The Scriptures are full of contradictions and ambiguities that beg for the clarifying light of reason. There is an interesting reciprocity here. What we make of reason or intellect is settled on the philosophical side. And whether we confidently accept the conclusions of philosophy or look upon them as illusory determines, first of all, whether we are open to Christianity, and, then, what kind of Christianity we embrace. The difference between Catholicism and much of Protestantism is determined by what is made of classical learning. A Von Harnack and his contemporary counterparts such as Leslie Dewart or Paul van Buren will decry the Hellenization of Christianity. Luther and Calvin both embraced a doctrine of the fall that lessened their confidence in natural intelligence. Both thought a natural theology impossible and were untroubled because they thought it unnecessary. For Luther and Calvin, faith is completely gratuitous; there is no rational preamble. In the words of Kierkegaard, "Faith is a leap into the dark."

Catholic spirituality centers on the Eucharist, but it doesn't begin there. What one thinks when one is on one's knees before the Eucharist depends on what one brings to the occasion. That one is upon one's knees before the tabernacle is the result of the assent given to a series of propositons which the believer holds to be true, e.g., that God is; that God is the creator of the universe; that man fell and was redeemed by the sacrificial act of the God-man, Christ; and that Christ founded a church and gave to it a priesthood with awesome power, including the power to consecrate. That bread becomes the body and blood of Christ requires the co-action of man and God. That all of this makes sense to the believer is due to a certain education, if you will. That these doctrines can be held by a rational person is due to the fact that they are consistent with experience and reason. The claim that Christ came in the fullness of time is not without justification. The intellect of the then civilized would had been prepared by centuries of Greek and Roman learning.

Reflecting on early Christian conceptions of learning, it is interesting to note that St. Benedict in composing his *Rule* had little to say about spiritual life, but it is clear that his *Rule* is designed to make that life possible. Benedict's asceticism is tempered compared to that of the Desert Fathers or to that of the Celts. It is an asceticism within the reach of a much greater number, largely because Benedict recognized the role which community plays in shaping the individual. A high priority is assigned to communal reading; table reading is, in fact, mandatory. Its end is the promotion of the interior life. Each monastery is to have a library and an archive; chronicles are to be kept. Within Benedict's own lifetime, monasteries became centers of learning, and were soon famous for their *scriptoria* where the classics of antiquity were copied for posterity. The librarian is specifically enjoined by the *Rule* to acquire new works. This attitude toward learning had important and lasting effects. The great monasteries became the cultural centers of Europe. Independent schools emerged in the abbeys, each seeking to outrival the others by increasing its library, by attracting professors of renown, and by drawing students to its intellectual tournaments. These schools promoted the study of the sciences and were to create a legion of remarkable theologians, philosophers, lawyers and scientists. We need but cite the schools of Cluny, Citeaux, Bec, Aurillac, St. Martin and St. Omer. A roll call of the leading scholars of the age, from Gregory through Bede, Lanfranc and Anselm, would name the abbots of many of those monasteries. The twelfth century Benedictine, Bernard of Clairvaux, became an author almost against his will as monks clamored for the text of his homilies. His books and monographs grew out of lectures recorded by fellow monks who circulated them sometimes without his knowledge and often without his editorial scrutiny. A Brother Godfrey asks him to write about the virtue of humility and the result is *De Gradibus Humilitatis*. Such books are part of our intellectual and spiritual heritage. With Sertillanges we can say: "Contact with genius is one of the choice graces that God grants to humble thinkers." But the availability of this heritage is not to be taken for granted. There are alternative conceptions of the religious life which militate against it.

The nineteenth century Protestant theologian, Albrecht Ritschl, reminds us of important differences between the traditional Catholic mind and the spirit of the Protestant Reformers. Of Protestantism he says, "Essentially a religion of action, (it) is hostile to both monasticism and asceticism. Abandoning the contemplative ideal, it substitutes in its place the standard of practical moral duty." This difference in emphasis is frequently overlooked by contemporary Catholic thinkers who have themselves substituted social work and counseling for theological inquiry and contemplation. Who has not heard it said, "What men think about God is of little importance as long as they live up to their social and moral ideals." Contrast that if you will with the dictum of St. Bonaventure, "If you wish to contemplate the invisible traits of God insofar as they belong to the unity of his essence, fix your gaze upon Being itself." For many, belief and theology are no longer the central features of the religious life. Almost without notice religion has degenerated into a man-centered enterprise of moral concern and healing.

It should never be forgotten that the primary aim in making life comfortable for others is to enable them, too, to lead the interior life. The greatest service which we can render others is to introduce them to the storehouse of Christian wisdom which gives life meaning. The pursuit of that wisdom is compatible with the acquisition of those skills which enable the subject through his labor to transform materials into economic resources. The impulse to beneficence has to be rightly directed. The active life is rudderless without the contemplative mind at its helm. We should never allow a false ecumenism to blur contradictory modes of approach. There are real differences between a Catholic outlook and a Protestant or secular perspective. As Sertillanges reminds us: "The choice of an intellectual father is always a serious thing." Respect for the contemplative life, whether it be led within the distracting chaos of urban life or within a secluded cloister in the countryside is a distinguishing mark of the Church. If, indeed, the contemplative way has been neglected in favor of an active life and one pursued largely for material goals, then the Bernards and Theresas among us ought to speak. No matter life's fortunes, there is available to all that serenity which comes with contemplation and adoration before the Eucharist: this ought to be said and often.

Response:
The Need for the Church
by
Joseph Schwartz

In his paper Dean Jude Dougherty emphasizes three points in the development of the interior life: (1) the requirement of the critical intelligence, (2) the need for learning, and (3) the need for the Church. It is the third point -- the need for the Church -- which I would like to develop in reference to higher education.

The Church is needed to provide spiritual direction for the college and university so that it, in turn, can provide spiritual direction for its students. Cardinal Newman defines the "spiritual life" as "obedience to a lawgiver, not a mere feeling or taste, and more than adherence to a moral code." This suggests the opposite of self-introspection and self-invention -- the opposite of sentimentality or taste. The Church as Lawgiver in the person of our Holy Father (message to the 1979 NCEA Convention) said: "...the crystal clear goal of Catholic education is above all a question of communicating Christ, of helping to form Christ in the lives of others."

It has been accepted in modern times that Catholic education unashamedly aims at locating the message of Christ proclaimed by the lawgiving Church at the very heart of the entire educational endeavor. "In this day," Newman said, "the Church's sway is contracted, but what she gained is a direct command and a reliable influence over her own institutions, which was wanting in the middle ages. A university is her possession in these times, as well as her creation." Newman would have been shocked by the deliberations of the infamous Land O'Lakes Conference (1967) that a University could put the Church at its fringe, go its own way, and still identify itself as Catholic. In 1975, addressing the heads of Jesuit universities around the world, Paul VI was clearly critical of institutions which lessened their Catholic character. He emphasized the need for complete doctrinal orthodoxy and fidelity to the Holy See. In the United States, however, Jesuit administrators still remain in the forefront of efforts to separate institutions of higher learning from the Church and its spiritual direction. St. Ignatius had quite a different view from many of those who bear the name of the order be founded. The study of theology was encouraged by St. Ignatius especially to promote piety. For him, it formed the intellectual basis of religious practice. It was "...the means most suitable to aiding our fellow men to the salvation of their souls."

Cardinal Newman saw that 19th century humanistic education with its moralistic emphasis was unable to give its students spiritual direction (and was thus incomplete), because it, in itself, lacked spiritual direction from an outer, more powerful, transcendental source.

It is true that Newman loved his 19th century humanistic education at Oxford. In fact, he used it, in part, as a model for the projected Catholic University in Ireland. Such an education made it clear that knowledge, an end in itself, is not virtue, and that confusing the two does a dis-service to both. Liberal education by itself creates a gentleman with tact, taste, cultivated intellect, and equitable mind. It is well to be a gentleman, since such a person has *prima facie* the advantage of having his mind drawn away from the things which could harm it -- not such a slight thing as it might seem. Newman wrote:

> Fastidiousness, though arguing no high principle..., nor sure in its operation, yet will often or generally be lively enough to create an absolute loathing of certain offences.

The "besetting sin" of such an education, however, is that the spiritual life is unattended; conscience is only a moral sense; the command of duty is mere taste; sin (if it exists) is not an offense against God but against human nature. The unwrinkled self-confidence students acquire lead to cold self-satisfaction, or the wish for death, as was the case of Oliver Alden in George Santayana's *The Last Puritan*.

Newman sharply criticizes this education. He asks "Shall we sharpen and refine the youthful intellect, and then leave it to exercise its new powers without direction? Or shall we proceed to feed it with divine truth, as it gains an appetite for knowledge?" Newman answers his own questions by reminding his readers that when Scripture promises us that the Commandments will be easy, it couples that promise with the charge that we must seek God early, remembering the Creator "in the days of your youth." St. Ignatius held that each professor should take care of the spiritual welfare of his students, inspiring them to the love and service of God.

In our own day, George Steiner is a much sharper critic of education which lacks a spiritual center. There is very little evidence, he holds, that humanistic studies humanize. T.S. Eliot was clearly correct, Steiner thinks, in his view that education no longer has a center. He maintains that classic values on a purely immanent, secular basis cannot replace the transcendent absolute which gave education its meaning.

The Church provides spiritual direction in that it settles the question of individualism, i.e., the dread argument of the individual case. Until that is settled, spiritual life is all but impossible. The question of whether we measure ourselves against being or the other way around, as Flannery O'Connor put it, remains the central question. The Church by teaching commitment to God as the fullness of being gives education spiritual direction. What knowledge is most worth having? That knowledge which possesses the most being, answers Francis Wade, S.J. God is the fullness of being; sacred or natural knowledge of him holds the highst place in Catholic education; and everything else comes in its order. In specifying the true image of man, Catholic education protects the student from both over-weaning pride and dehumanization.

The Church teaches the school a healthy respect for mystery, and ultimately for the sacred. Either we learn the centrality of the sacred or we will be trivialized by our solipsism. The Incarnation is the end and the beginning of our being -- the only source of poise and serenity. It is more than mere historical fact that the Church is the mother of the University.

The Church's Spiritual Mission to the Poor
by
Fr. Bruce Ritter, OFM

One of the dumbest things I ever did was to accept the invitation to address this illustrious group. Whatever weak and illusory pretensions I ever had to the scholarly life disintegrated forever when the honesty and authenticity of my students at Manhattan College forced me to seek refuge in the slums of the East Village almost 19 years ago.

You see, by training I am -- or was -- an academician -- I have a doctorate in late medieval history of dogma. The topic of my thesis was an arcane one: the debate over the abstruse mysteries of the Filioque -- whether the Holy Spirit proceeded from the Father and the Son, or from the Father through the Son.

Make no mistake about it: it was a matter of furious and sometimes violent debate between East and West, between the Orthodox Churches of Constantinople and the Latin Churches of Rome. This debate has allegedly separated the Churches, divided Christendom, for centuries.

I say "allegedly" because I had iconoclastically set out to demonstrate that the real issue was one of spiritual jurisdictions and temporal power: that the real issue discussed, debated, and argued for more than two years in the last great, truly ecumenical gathering of the whole Church -- in the Council of Florence in 1437, was not the Trinity but the Primacy of Rome over the Eastern Churches. I haven't seen that historic dissertation in over twenty years and I doubt now that I would recognize it if I happened to stumble over it.

Because my students at Manhattan couldn't tolerate my self-righteous exhortation to zeal and commitment -- not seeing any of these exalted virtues in my own life -- they cavalierly invited me to practice what I preached. What's more, I received that coercive invitation in the middle of a homily I was delivering to about 400 college students while celebrating Sunday Mass on campus.

I asked for a new assignment: to live and work among the poor. I didn't know at the time that I was abandoning forever my pursuit of the scholarly life.

Six street kids, all under 16, invaded my space and life at 2:00 am one February morning in the middle of a raging blizzard. Fleeing from some junkies who were pimping them and who had just forced them to make a porn film, they had knocked on the door of my East Village Apartment and asked if they could sleep on the floor. What could I do?

"Don't worry," one of the kids said, "we know you're a priest and we'll be good and stay away from the girls and you can go to sleep in peace in your bed." I thanked him for that courtesy.

The next morning this kid went outside and brought back four more kids. "This is the rest of us," he said, "the rest of our 'family.' They were afraid to come last night; they wanted us to check you out first. I told them that you didn't come on to us last night and that it was probably o.k..."

That was the beginning of Covenant House. I couldn't find any child care agency that would touch these kids -- they were all young prostitutes and hustlers -- so I kept them. (I figured the ancient law of the open range that allowed a cowboy to keep as his own any unaccompanied wandering calf -- mavericks -- applied to the concrete canyons and asphalt trails of New York City. Besides, there was no law south of 14th Street and east of Avenue A).

The next day two more kids, two more mavericks, came in ... And the next day two more. The word got around real fast about that dumb priest who didn't have the guts to kick you out...

But the fact that I have been outside the scholarly precincts for almost 20 years is not the only reason why it was just stupid of me to accept this invitation to speak to you tonight. The first rule of public speaking is to know your audience, and the second is like unto it: at least say a few things in words and accents peculiar to academic discourse they might agree with.

I don't know the words any more. And I'm not sure that I can say anything that you either haven't heard a thousand times before, or that isn't patently self-evident -- or that you won't disagree with violently. If I do say anything that offends I beg you to ascribe my lapse to a lack of insight, a certain narrowness of vision and not to any deliberate desire to be provocative.

The problem is of course that my subject matter is an almost indecently impossible one: The Church's spiritual mission to the poor.

Let me call upon the poorly remembered shreds of my academic training in Rome more than 27 years ago and engage in a little *explicatio terminorum* before I raise the crucial question.

By the poor in this context I refer to the physically, materially, economically deprived poor, the victims of structural poverty, economic exploitation. I refer to the chronically homeless, chronically hungry, chronically disadvantaged and alienated. They can be sharecroppers in Louisiana, migrant workers in our 50 states, millions of undocumented aliens eking out a bare existence, the millions of people raised to adulthood in refugee camps... We are a people who like to describe unhappy realities with a bowdlerized language so we often call them merely the "disconnected" or "unconnected" or even the "underclass."

They are the *anewim* of the gospel, the beloved of Jesus. I refer to most of the world's population.

By "Spiritual mission to the poor," I obviously refer to the principle work of the Church to "preach the gospel to the poor," to evangelize them, to reveal to them the beauty and glory of the kingdom of God present among them by making Jesus Christ real and visible and present and concrete among them.

By "Church" I refer to our institutional hierarchical Church that Pope Paul VI claims, with appeals to scripture and tradition, bears the principal responsibility and authority for the evangelization of all peoples -- and, most especially, the duty of preaching the gospel to the poor.

Having defined, or rather described, somewhat loosely the terms of our discussion, may I now raise the obvious and critical question --indeed, one of the most troubling questions of our time: is the Church fast losing, if it has not already largely lost, its ability to proclaim the gospel in words and ways the poor can understand?

That happened in the Middle Ages when a decadent and intellectually arid scholasticism, and the preoccupation of the Church with questions of authority and power -- both secular and spiritual -- seemed to exhaust almost entirely its energies. The poor were not being preached to -- parish life was in almost total disrepair. So were the walls of the Church that appeared so solid and impregnable but that were actually falling down -- because the gospel was not being preached. It was being studied to death. It was being dissected by scholars and clerics. It was being chewed up and categrized by logic and exegetes. It had become the intellectual plaything for brilliant academics... But it was not being preached.

Clearly St. Francis didn't really understand that when he first heard that message from the crucifix at San Damiano: "Francis, go, rebuild my church which is falling down..."

The problem with St. Francis was, of course, that he was a literalist. Taking the voice of the Lord literally, he started rebuilding little chapels abandoned for generations, scrounging rocks from the hillside, and help from his wealthy young friends.

As a literalist, when he read the gospel: "Go, sell all you have, give it to the poor and come follow me...," he did exactly that. He may have cursed a bit and sworn at an unforseen fate, but he did it. He threw off his clothes, and, abandoning all his considerable possessions, walked naked into our history and our hearts.

As a literalist, when he read in the gospels that to preach the gospel was to preach Christ, he did exactly that. And he did it in the manner that Christ commanded his disciples; he took a companion; going without shoes and staff and money; only one tunic; caring not a whit about where he would sleep or what he would eat -- or even that he would be listened to.

Francis knew, maybe God taught him, that the gospel taught you how to preach the gospel. He knew that the way you preached the gospel was at least as important as what you preached. He knew then what everybody has always known and what Pope Paul VI reminds us of once again in his Apostolic Exhortation: *Evangelii Nuntiandi*, "On Evangelization in the Modern World:" "Modern man listens more willingly to witnesses than to teachers, and if he does listen to teachers, it is because they are witnesses..." Francis knew that to preach the gospel was to preach the incarnation: Jesus Christ, Son of God, crucified. He knew that in order to preach the gospel, whether to the poor or the rich, he had to be poor, to be known as poor.

Pope Paul VI is quite correct, I believe, in perceiving that the central drama of our time is the "split between the gospel and our culture" and "that every effort must be made to ensure a full evangelization of culture, or more correctly of cultures, They have to be regenerated by an encounter with the gospel. But this encounter will not take place if the Gospel is not proclaimed."

The gospel tells us that the gospel is proclaimed more by lifestyle and witness than by words, teaching, explanation or a library full of Apostolic Exhortations.

Our modern Church finds this truth troublesome and infinitely disturbing.

The truth is, of course, that we, the modern Church, are a comfortable, middle class, wealthy church, more at home with techniques and methods and training programs about evangelization than we are with letting the gospel teach us how to preach the Incarnation.

To a certain extent, perhaps, we are witnessing the remanifestation of an old heresy; indeed, the primeval heresy of the Christian Church, that once was called Docetism. It was, in short a denial of the physical human reality of Christ. Christ was real alright but not in any truly categorically human sense. It was too undignified to think of Christ with actual hands and feet and toenails and armpits.

The majesty of God could not be permitted to be defiled in such a way. It merely "seemed" (from the Greek dokeo/dokein: to seem) to us that Jesus was a man. In actuality his body was imaginary, made of star dust perhaps or moon beams. But it was not real and concrete. Jesus's body didn't get dirty. It was too unseemly.

This heresy served many useful purposes, one of which was to push God back out of the way, to disentangle him from our own guts, our own flesh and blood. It kept God at a comfortable distance and the world comfortably secular. It was, of course, in essence a denial of the Incarnation.

In that same apostolic exhortation, "On Evangelization," in which Paul VI describes the split between gospel and culture as the central drama of our time, he suggests also that the phenomenon of secularism is the most striking characteristic of our modern culture:

> Here we are thinking of a true secularism: a concept of the world according to which the latter is self-explanatory, without any need for recourse to God, who thus becomes superfluous and an encumbrance. This sort of secularism, in order to recognize the power of man, therefore, ends up by doing without God and even by denying him.
>
> New forms of atheism seem to flow from it: a man-centered atheism, no longer abstract and metaphysical but pragmatic, systematic and militant. Hand in hand with this atheistic secularism, we are daily faced, under the most diverse forms, with a consumer society, the pursuit of pleasure set up as the discrimination of every kind...

Has this militant secularism, born in part from a renascent docetism with its consequent weakening of the sense of the passionate, physical reality and physical presence of Jesus as Son of God, permeated modern Christianity? And is it -- this loss of the sense and truth of the Incarnation -- at least in part responsible for this split between gospel and culture? And is it not quite inevitable, therefore, that we would create and formulate to express our less than robust sense of the beauty and glory of the Incarnation, a somewhat bloodless, sanitized liturgy, lacking passion and power, a liturgy that speaks neither to the rich nor the poor?

If indeed the *lex orandi* is the *lex credendi* -- if indeed, the way we pray and worship is the measure of our faith, then the pallid liturgy of our Western Church is an exceedingly poor instrument to preach a Christ present and real and passionate among us. It is certainly not a liturgy in tune with the simple pieties and profound needs of the poor. Nor is our generally feckless state of preaching, of proclamation of the good news. Christ and Francis preached the good news with fire and conviction and authority because they were men of passion and conviction -- and they preached the gospel with unassailable credentials: they were poor.

Do we really think that St. Francis would be welcome in many --perhaps most -- of our parishes today? And, if we did take the chance and invite him to preach to us, would we understand his words, could we deal with his poverty? It would not be easy to tolerate this cheerful infinitely colorful beggar in our midst.

We not only present the gospel poorly in our liturgies and

frequently preach it without passion, we even preach it from the wrong pulpit, at the wrong time, in the wrong words.

Paul VI reminds us that modern man is sated by talk, tired of listening, and what is worse, almost impervious to words. We are aware, Paul VI, continues, "that many psychologists and sociologists think that man has passed beyond the civilization of the word, which is now ineffective and useless, and that today he lives in the civilization of the image."

If that be true, and it certainly is at the very least substantially true, then the implications for the preaching of the gospel are profound:

When you talk about the vision of the gospel, most especially when you're talking about it to the poor, you have to talk about it in simple ways, using simple words and understand what your vision of the gospel means, it helps to express its inner reality in simple parables that assault the mind with their special kind of inescapable logic.

Nobody, ever, didn't understand what the parable of the Good Samaritan meant.

If the Pope is correct, namely that we have moved from a civilization of the word to a civilization of the image, then the best way to preach and proclaim the gospel, most especially to the poor, is through provocative, self-validating, powerfully convincing images --exactly like those of the gospel -- and that the best means to do this in our culture is through the electronic media, most especially television. (Very few of the poor show up in our churches: they practically all have television sets).

Yet, the Church that practically invented religious broadcasting has for all practical purposes almost abandoned it. The Catholic Church has never really developed, has never really seized its opportunities to develop, the effective preachers and communicators needed by this no longer new media.

And so who so often preaches the gospel on television? And often brings the gospel into disrepute and ridicule? Men who sell indulgences for money or who preach a self-indulgent spiritual happiness or who thunder out apocalyptic warnings about the devil, who create instant miracles in exchange for contributions...

If there is a split between the gospel and our culture, the men and women of our culture are not totally to blame. At best we can speak of a mutual abandonment.

The problem with this central drama of our time with this split between gospel and culture is that it devastates the concept and reality of Catholicism.

The very idea of the universality of the Roman Catholic Church

-- as universal -- becomes almost, but no quite, a contradiction in terms. By very definition, our 20th century culture and cultures are in fact the very masses of people necessary to constitute and create a true universality. The price one pays therefore for this gospel/culture split is a limited catholicity at best, and one that runs the grave risk of limited catholicity at best, and one that runs the grave risk of being more and more defined by ideology and dogma and orthodoxy than by the universal preaching of the gospel of Jesus. In short, the universal church inevitably takes on more and more of the characteristics of a sect.

If the institutional Church is to preach the gospel to a culture foreign to it, separate from it, alienated from it, the Church itself, not the culture, must bridge the gap by incarnating the divine in that culture.

The challenge that St. Francis, quite unknowingly, I believe, presented to the church at its very highest level was to reunite gospel and culture. All he did was to ask, in 1209, if he and a few friends could be permitted, in union with the Church, to live out the gospel literally as Christ lived it, among the poor, so that he could preach the gospel of his Lord Jesus Christ.

Innocent III, a towering figure of the 13th century papacy to whom Francis made the request, was not impressed. About to refuse Francis on the grounds that such a feat was humanly impossible, he was dissuaded by Cardinal John Colonna who argued that such a refusal might itself be contrary to the gospel and a devastating precedent in the Church. Could the Church actually refuse to p ermit, to authorize, to support, to encourage, men and women of the Church to follow the gospel as Christ himself lived it?

What a classic example of the conflict between institution and vision. And what a classic example of the power of the Holy Spirit protecting and guiding its Church from error. The Holy Spirit made Innocent III say yes. To have done otherwise, I think, would have been to deny the possibility of the Incarnation of Jesus Christ, Savior, in our human culture.

But isn't that always the perennial problem of institutions? They're always getting in the way and messing up the vision under the guise of preserving it.

The problem with noble vision, on the other hand, is that they are extremely fragile -- the stuff of dreams, gossamer creations...

If you want to safeguard and nurture a vision you have to formalize it, to undergird it with structure, to express its inner reality with pragamatic policies and procedures -- in one dreadful word: to institutionalize it!

If you do that, of course, you inevitably kill off half of the vision, crushing, besmirching; defiling its purity. That is the simple truth of it.

The other equally simple and compelling truth is that if you don't institutionalize the vision you destroy it: it will simply die, it will go away. The vision will cease to exist.

We should never be discouraged if occasionally the institution gets in our way. It will always be there to do exactly that. Our job is not to let the institution so permeate and control the vision that the vision itself simply begins to wither.

Is it possible, that, as St. Francis seems to demonstrate, only those who become poor for the sake of the gospel can really preach the gospel to the poor?

Is it possible that this split between gospel and culture, so bemoaned by Paul VI, is largely of our own making? Is it possible that the pallid and passionless and unreal incarnation lived by most of us have created a Christ made of star dust and moon beams that serves mostly to beautify the stained glass windows of our cathedrals?

It may be that middle class evangelists cannot preach the gospel, that they can only teach doctrine.

Until the gospel of an incarnate Christ is preached to the poor with fire and passion and conviction, the true catholicity of the Church will lie wounded somewhere in the gap between our culture and the gospel.

What the final outcome will be of, in Pope Paul VI's words, that "central drama of our time" is certainly not clear to me, perhaps not to any of us.

Catholic is supposed to mean universal.

Catholic is supposed to mean that nobody is excluded, most especially the poor.

Jesus had a hard time making that point. He still does. Just about all his friends -- and certainly most of his enemies --wanted to make Jesus sectarian.

His friends and enemies alike didn't want him to associate with lepers or Samaritans, or publicans or sinners -- or even women. The disciples of John and Jesus had their own turf battles over who were greater... And everybody thought it was OK to hate the Romans.

If you want to hate somebody or to exclude them from your company, or make yourself better than they are, you can always find some religious, economic, social, ethnic or historical reason to do so.

When Jesus finally -- with some impatience, I think -- taught us who was going to make it into his kingdom, he did so without reference to doctrinal or sectarian conditions.

He said very clearly that it was mercy -- not doctrine; pity --not dogma; love -- not creedal statements that got you into his company.

He said we are welcome into his kingdom if we feed the hungry, clothe the naked, shelter the homeless, comfort the afflicted... in short, if we preach the gospel to the anewim, the beloved poor of Jesus. And, if we don't do these things, we're not welcome.

Far too often good and well-meaning men and women have tried to exclude others from their love on the basis of doctrine or race or money or for dozens of other reasons.

We widen the gap between gospel and culture that way.

We make ourselves and the Church uncatholic that way.

Love doesn't exclude anybody from the kingdom of God, most especially the poor who are its primary and rightful citizens.

The matter is a serious one. The question may very well be that the Church can no longer easily incarnate the Godhead in a secular society.

To the extent that the Church falters in its mission to evangelize the poor, it withdraws from its primary spiritual mission to preach the Incarnation of Jesus Christ Savior. Pallid liturgies, deckless, passionless preaching in a largely unintelligible language by the people of the culture of the word to a people of the culture of the image, can only further the secularization of our culture and deepen the abyss between gospel and culture.

The implications for the catholicity of the Church are profound -- and its impact on the Church profound.

The Church inevitably appears and acts more and more sectarian as it drifts ever farther apart from the culture that provides its living matrix. And it is quite evident that the signs of sectarianism in our Church are distressingly real today. I only need to mention a growing preoccupation with revealed truth as dogma, with credal formulations, and a growing tendency on the part of some to believe that dogmas and doctrines and creed can be shoehorned and crowbarred into docile minds by discipline or fear of the consequences of dissent.

Francis had some limitations. He freely admitted them and his confreres were not blind to them. One limitation that he enshrined in his Rule was a certain mistrust of learning and scholarship. He rather peremptorily ordered his friars that those who were unlettered should not seek to become so -- lest the spirit of learning extinguish the spirit of prayer...

At the same time, however, he eagerly welcomed scholars into his community -- men such as St. Anthony and St. Bonaventure -- two of the most illustrious doctors of the Church to preach, to teach, to educate...

The great universities of Europe were soon staffed by members of my Franciscan Order -- and we gloried in the delights of debate as much as our ability to preach the gospel to the poor. Duns Scotus was as famous for the complexity and brilliance of his theology as he was for the simplicity and limpid clearness of his sermons to the uneducated.

Perhaps the scholars and academicians of the 13th and 14th centuries -- despite an unseemly over-preoccupation with the life of the mind -- have an important lesson to teach us about the need not only to stand within a well defined intellectual tradition but the need as well, to engage in vigorous, free debate: to discuss, to argue, to contest.

I am not certain that a well-defined American Catholic intellectual tradition exists. Nor am I certain that there exists an adequate number of eager, vocal champions of our Catholic heritage willing and able to debate the fiercely contested issues of our times.

We can all appreciate the problems bishops are faced with when the average Catholic in our pews simply does not understand the issues and can therefore be substantially mislead about what the magisterium considers authentic teaching -- particularly if the teaching proceeds from an articulate, persuasive credentialled Catholic spokesman.

The bishops, as guardians of authentic teaching, face another extraordinarily difficult challenge: how to deal with theological debate and theological dissent in a society so dominated by the electronic media that every half-completed thought, every partial insight, every untested theory is tried out on *Good Morning America* or *Meet the Press*.

In their role as guardians and teachers of authentic doctrine revealed by Christ through his Church, the bishops also have, especially today, the difficult and unenviable task of calling forth in the Church the skilled and articulate spokesmen capable of a convincing defense of the teaching of the magisterium.

If the Church does lack these trained, skillful champions, then it faces an infinitely more serious crisis than the teaching of dissident theologians. It is a massive crisis of both internal and external credibility that almost calls into question the Church's ability to preach the gospel to anybody -- least of all the poor.

The sterile intellectual lucubrations of the 14th century theologians lacked relevance precisely because they so clearly demonstrated the almost absolute separation between gospel and culture.

The equally sterile debates of East and West at the Council of Ferrara-Florence, purportedly also in defense of doctrinal purity, were carried on at great expense for several years over the wrong issues and for the wrong purposes, while the urgent and compelling needs of the Latin Church were ignored.

A renowned scholar of the work of the Council of Florence, Fr. Joseph Gill, S.J., observed that if the time, the money, the energy expended on the search for an illusory and essentially political union of East and West had instead been directed toward the urgently needed spiritual renewal of the Latin Church, the Protestant Reformation that occurred 100 years later might not have been necessary.

The Church's mission to the poor is to preach the gospel, to evangelize, that is, to make Christ real and present and concrete and visible: to make the Incarnation happen all over again in our society.

If the Church would call us back to the work of the Incarnation, if the Church would have us take the risk of making Christ present among the poor, then it must accept as its own the violence and ugliness and pain and alienation and discomfort that are the very flesh and blood of the poor and the only body that Christ will find worthy to inhabit and which he will bring back to the Father.

In this journey with and among the poor the Church will realize its identity as the "pilgrim church" -- and, I think, on this journey with and among the anewim, the poor of Jesus, the Church can only be the ecclesia semper reformanda: the Church always needing reformation, the Church always being reformed.

It is a foregone conclusion that the Church will do this. Christ made it clear the he would never let the Church fail in its primary mission which is to preach the gospel to the poor -- the only sure and certain sign that the kingdom of God has been established. In that sense we can glory in the indefectibility of his Church while we passionless conscripts in his kingdom wait and wonder when he will speak to another passionate young man praying before a crucifix to the message: Go, rebuild my Church.

Response:
by
Charles Dechert

Certainly Fr. Ritter's topic, "The Church's Spiritual Mission to the Poor," is somewhat overwhelming -- and as a product of the Seraphicum, he appropriately began with a series of definitions: touching the poor as the "physically, materially, economically deprived" -- the "disconnected" or "unconnected" or even the underclass. Certainly Fr. Ritter's own experience has given him an intimate familiarity with the most exploited and deprived of our urban population, but also with the most ruthless exploiters who may themselves be deprived; he can truly speak of the "violence, ugliness and pain" of poverty -- but are they "integral?" Is not simple and austere poverty possible?

In a world of limited resources, restrictions on consumption are inevitable; yet, for most of the world's population today, inadequate levels of nutrition and housing, education and health are principally a product of institutional inadequacies and structural failures -- apart from the malice of power politics manipulating famine and human needs, or the greed that puts everything on sale, the buying and selling of souls. Fr. Ritter has spent much of his adult life trying to mend the wretched, twisted products of such malice. But we must avoid the temptation to equate poverty with moral anarchy -- the phrase "pauper sed honestus" -- "poor but honorable," characterizing the family status of so many saints, is no mere formula. But poverty bureaucratically defined in merely monetary terms is also most misleading, especially in America.

Certainly the Christian's mission to the poor must include the provision of material and spiritual needs (the works of mercy) as integral to evangelization and "conversion of life." so often now we forget that Christianity does have a moral code; that there are criteria of good and bad behavior; that social virtues and a life in accordance with right reason are enjoined by that tradition; that Christian societies have, by and large, manifested strong and productive family units, good public order, general satisfaction of basic human needs, and a community spirit capable of dealing rigorously with moral anarchy.

In addition to those activities directed at mitigating the plight of the poor, clearly the Christian should encourage healthy social structures -- a difficult task in a pluralistic society that acknowledges consensually few moral limits, in which some leaders will exploit injustices, discontents and vices in the pursuit of power at the expense of souls.

Father Ritter has spoken of this gnostic pursuit of power, of a secularization based on a denial of the Incarnation, of a God too remote to make any difference. Equally to be feared is a gnostic insistence on the intrinsic evil of matter and the unique value of the spirit. This, too, may result in moral nihilism and the disintegration of the social fabric.

The love of neighbor enjoined by Christ is indeed manifested by good words -- but these good words must be informed by truth in order to bear the fruit of social structural reform in the interest of man's temporal well-being and eternal salvation. St. Francis provided a response to the Manichean gnosis, which was not devoid of good works but was fundamentally erosive of society and good order. His poverty detached him and his followers from the motivational handles employed by Power. His obedience to the Church ensured his orthodoxy. His love of nature and his fellowmen was a reaffirmation of the goodness of God's material creation and a response to the *bonhommes* whose errors might well have wrecked a civilization. His was an affirmation of the goodness of things well and constructively ordered.

Response:
by
Francis Canavan, S.J.

It would be easy for me to say simply that I second what Fr. Ritter for the work he has done and is doing here in New York. He has carried since I am supposed to sing for my supper, I must deliver myself of a song.

The first stanza of the song has to be a paean of praise of Fr. Ritter for the work he had done and is doing here in New York. He has carried the gospel to those who are not only poor but are ruthlessly exploited and degraded by others, and he has done this not only in word but, by what really counts, deed. He demonstrates a living faith in Christ by what he does for the Lord's least brethren. It is by this that he, like us, will ultimately be judged.

I am called upon, however, to comment on his words and I will therefore suggest some nuances that might appropriately be added to his text. First, the *anewim* of the gospel are not only "the chronically homeless, chronically hungry, chronically disadvantaged," but all the poor and lowly of the Lord, many of whom are adequately fed, clothed and sheltered, but are, nonetheless, not among the great and favored ones of the earth. Secondly, while it is true that the Church fails if she does not bring the gospel and its message of hope to them, she cannot confine herself to bringing it only to them or simply divorce herself from the aspirations of human culture.

The gospel is radical in its demands, and men like St. Francis of Assisi have generously responded to those demands. But the radical tradition in Christianity has its limitations. Professor Clarke E. Cochran of Texas Tech University has well remarked:

> The same Father who sent Jesus to show a new way also created the world and human beings with a need for order, culture, and stability. Those who would transform the world forget that Jesus recommended no specific plan of political change, no form of a regime, and no social-economic theory. The radical gospel sits side by side with the prudent advice of Romans 13, Jesus' evasive answer to the tribute question, and the compromise over the application of the law to gentile Christians (Acts 15: 1-29). ["The Radical Gospel and Christian Prudence," in Francis Canavan, ed., *The Ethical Dimension of Political Life* (Durham, N.C.: Duke University Press, 1983), pp. 191-192].

The preferential option for the poor which the Church is now stressing is meant to correct our all too human tendency to leave the poor out of the benefits of society, but we should be wary also of the opposite tendency to regard the poor as the only legitimate claimants on those benefits.

As Bishop Egan said last night and Fr. Ritter has repeated today, the Church on the eve of the Reformation was overintellectualized and overinstitutionalized. That is, in fact, a perennial danger. St. Jerome, a millenium before, had worried lest God call him a Ciceronian rather than a Christian. There has always been a strain of feeling in Catholicism that denounces overintellectualism and emphasizes the very Catholic truth that faith without works is dead and understanding that does not lead to practice is sterile: *non in dialectica statuit Deus salvare hominem*, as St. Anselm said. But this reaction, healthy though it is, carries its own danger with it, which is that of running off into anti-intellectualism and mere activism. The Church, in fact, needs both a head and a heart.

The heart has its reasons that reason does not know, as Pascal said, and we must never forget that because, without the reasons of the heart, there is no faith. But the heart that cuts itself off from reason ceases to be Catholic and lapses into that sentimentalism which is probably the most prevalent heresy of our time. I am inclined, therefore, to think that Fr. Ritter may exaggerate when he says that contemporary Catholicism "runs the grave risk of being more and more defined by ideology and dogma and orthodoxy than by the universal preaching of the gospel of Jesus." On this proposition several comments are necessary.

First, it is a mistake to identify -- or even to seem to identify --dogma and orthodoxy with ideology. Ideology is a program of political action disguised as an explanation of the nature of the world and society. Its purpose is to draw people into the service of a political cause so that the ideologues may win political power and so be able to remake society. Dogma, on the other hand, is a definition of revealed truth, whether it has any relevance to political action or not, and orthodoxy is the correct teaching of that truth.

Now, I do not see how anyone can preach the gospel of Jesus Christ without being prepared to answer questions about him. The first and most obvious of these questions is, "Who is this Jesus?" It renders the preaching of the gospel ineffective if we duck this question and take refuge in a vagueness that leaves the hearers uncertain whether Jesus was anything more than a man, how he came into the world, whether he really died for our sins, rose again, and will come again at the end of time to judge the living and the dead. The only effective way of preaching the gospel, I should think, is to start with a clear and certain answer to the question, "Who is Jesus?" *and this means dogma*:

> We believe in one Lord, Jesus Christ, the only Son of God, eternally begotten of the Father, God from God, Light from Light, true God from true God, begotten, not made, one in Being with the Father, through whom all things were made. For us men and for our salvation he came down from heaven; by the power of the Holy Spirit he was born of the Virgin Mary, and became man. For our sake he was crucified under Pontius Pilate; he suffered, died, and was buried. On the third day he rose again in fulfillment of the

Scriptures; he ascended into heaven and is seated at the right hand of the Father. He will come again in glory to judge the living and the dead, and his kingdom will have no end.

Dogma, in turn, requires an institutional Church strong enough to define right doctrine against those who, pretending to explain who Jesus was, really explain him away. Faith without works indeed is dead, but a faith without an intellectually definable content becomes mere emotion. Theory is no substitute for practice, but practice has to be guided by theory in order to be sound practice. As Fr. Ritter says, we must not "...let the institution so permeate and control the vision that the vision itself simply begins to wither." Neither, on the other hand, must we let the vision run wild.

We live, after all, at the end of a century which has been devastated by visions run wild. Adolf Hitler is this century's most famous mass murderer but, if we judge by numbers alone, he was not its worst one. We may never know just how many people Stalin, Mao, and Pol Pot starved, shot, and beat to death, but the number runs at minimum into scores of millions. This was done in the name of a vision of universal brotherhood and a classless society in which all exploitation of man by man would disappear. Without vision the people perish, as the prophet said, but let us not overlook how many people have perished in this century because someone had a vision.

I am afraid I must simply disagree with Fr. Ritter when he tells us that Jesus "said very clealy that it was mercy -- not doctrine; pity -- not dogma; love -- not creedal statements that got you in his company." I do not find in the New Testament that Our Lord talked about these subjects at all. The object of his criticism was not doctrine but legalism, the preference for the letter of the law above its spirit. The doctrine, the dogma, and the creedal statements came after his death and were about him, and they are still the necessary means of keeping knowledge of who and what he was alive in the minds and hearts of men.

Finally, I am not so worried as Fr. Ritter about "a growing preoccupation with revealed truth as dogma, with creedal formulations, and a growing tendency on the part of some to believe that dogmas and doctrines and creeds can be shoehorned and crowbarred into docile minds by discipline and fear of the consequences of dissent." I mean no disparagement of those who have become famous as dissenting theologians. They are worthy and, I am told, charming men. But I see no reason to believe that they are any more concerned about the poor than the rest of us. On the contrary, the thrust of their dissent seems to identify them as spokesmen for the felt needs of that comfortable middle class which Fr. Ritter feels with some justification to be reluctant to hear the full gospel of Christ.

Let us admit it, we are all reluctant and slow to hear the gospel. At very best, we make some progress in the course of a lifetime in interiorizing its demands. Even then, we do it in a somewhat lopsided way. St. Francis of Assisi and St. Thomas Aquinas were among the greatest lights of Christian history, but they were very different men and we need them both, mind and heart, intellect and will, contemplation and action. Both, incidentally, were devoted sons of the Church and neither was noted for dissent.

Prayer and Meditation for Spiritual Life
by
Bishop Sean O'Malley, OFM Cap.

There is a recent revival of interest in spirituality after two decades of a different agenda. It is still premature to speak about a spiritual renewal. Upheaval over external change - as Cardinal Wright used to say, "rearranging the furniture" - coupled with a disintegration of catechesis, left many Catholics easy prey for the cults and fundamentalist religions. Last year in Rome, I listened in dismay to the conversations of our Indian Capuchins who spoke of thousands upon thousands of young American and Western Europeans who are wandering about the Indian subcontinent starving to death in pursuit of some spiritual enlightenment. Yes, starving, physically and spiritually.

We have failed to present to our young people the secrets of the interior life, the pursuit of an ideal, the mysticism of contemplation. There is a great hunger in contemporary society. Our freezers are full, but we keep the menu hidden from sight and we wonder why people are going to other restaurants rather than ours.

Spirituality for our times is not something new and original or based only on current Christian experience. The vital movements of recent origin all enjoy a continuity with universal Catholic tradition. Thus we see Charles de Foucald drawing on the desert Fathers and Carmelite mystics; Mons. Escriva on the Ignatian exercises; and Chiara Lubich on Franciscan tradition. In a similar way, the great spiritual movements of the Counter Reformation found their inspiration in the Middle Ages, John of the Cross read the Rheno-Flemish mystics of the Late Middle Ages -- Ruysbroeck, Meister Eckhart, and Tauler; St. Ignatius and St. Teresa nourished their ideas at the font of the *Devotio Moderna*.

Tragically, the great mystics are perceived as being out of date and exaggerated or unbalanced in their theological and anthropoligical presuppostions. We have replaced *The Dark Night of the Soul* with *I'm OK, You're OK*.

Our task as scholars and educators is to retrieve from their cultural trappings the Gospel values which the Christian mystics lived and wish to share with us. In so doing, we will discover that they were trying to live the same ideals that we do, that they had to face similar difficulties, temptations, and conflicts.

Spirituality is not, of course, a science to be studied but a way of life. As the *Imitation of Christ* says: "It is more important to feel compunction than to know how to define it." In the Catholic tradition, we look to the saints to help us discover the way to God. The saints are the true theologians who teach us about God and about friendship with God. Nikos Kazantzakis in his fictious biography of St. Francis includes a scene in which Francis is conversing with Brother Leo about Leo's special way of finding God:

> At first Brother Leo was reticent. Finally he confessed: "I was born lazy and that was my special way of finding God. If I had spent all my time studying and working and involved in many things, I might never have come to know God. But I liked to go out into the fields and see the flowers and the animals; and at night I looked at the sky and marveled at the beauty of the firmament and I asked myself, 'Where did all this come from?' And so my laziness helped me discover God.

We all need this "laziness" to find God. Before we put on our socks in the morning, we should know where, when, and how long we will pray - just as we know where and when we will eat. We need time and space for God: "Brother Leo's laziness." We must decide to dedicate time each day to prayer. We must establish a routine, a rule of life, a schedule that gives some prime time to prayer.

St. Teresa rightly affirmed that prayer is a matter of life and death for the Christian: it can never be replaced by anything else. In her *Vida*, she defines prayer as follows: "Nothing else than an intimate sharing between friends, it means taking time frequently to be alone with Him who we know loves us."

Father Larranaga writes: "The more we pray, the more we will want to pray." St. Augustine says it is like gravity pulling at an arrow - the closer the thing is to the center of gravity, the stronger the attraction, the greater speed.

In the same charming novel of Francis of Assisi, Kazantzakis provides a description of the inexorable attraction that drew the saint to God:

> St. Francis emerged from the cave after three days of prayer. He spoke to Brother Leo: "Until now they have used many names to describe God. Tonight I have discovered other ways of describing God - the unfathomable abyss, the insatiable, the indefatigable, the One who never says to a soul, 'That's enough.' "
>
> "Never enough," Francis shouted. "It is not enough, Brother Leo. That is what God has shouted at me during these three days and three nights - 'Never enough.' A poor man is made of clay and protests 'I cannot take any more,' and God replies, 'You can.' And the man sighs, 'I am going to burst.' God replies, 'Burst.' " Leo said, "What more can God ask of you, Francis? You kissed the leper."
>
> "Not enough." "You left your mother."
>
> "Not enough." "You made a spectacle of yourself, returning even the clothes on your back."
>
> "Not enough." "Aren't you the poorest man in the world?"

"It is not enough. Brother Leo, *God is never enough*."

If it is true that the more we pray, the more we will want to pray, - it is also true that the less we pray, the less we will want to pray. It is only in a life of prayer that we too can discover that God is never enough.

The interior life begins for religious, priest, or lay person when we make the firm, irrevocable decision that prayer is going to be a constant in our life. Prayer will help to give us a new vision of reality, the meaning of suffering, of love. "Love" is a commonplace in our lexicon. But what does it mean?

One of my favorite novels is Perez Galdos' *Marianela*. It is a story about a wonderful girl with a great capacity to love. Marianela has a boyfriend who is blind: his name is Pablo. Marianela works and sacrifices and borrows money to be able to send Pablo to the city for an operation that finally restores his vision. When Pablo discovers that Marianela is a plain-looking girl, he leaves her for someone else. The great irony of the story is that whe Pablo was blind he was better able to see Marianela's true beauty.

Sometimes it is only the cross and suffering that allows us to truly experience love. Too often, like the beneficiaries of the multiplication of the loaves, we are so fascinated with the gifts that we forget the giver, the *love*. We need spiritual vision to see beyond the material things, to see the value of the Cross. This vision sees sin present in human reality. This is the realism of the mystics. In his *Noche Oscura*, St. John writes: "The first and chief benefit of this dry and dark night of contemplation is the knowledge of one's self and of one's own misery." Elsewhere, he continues:

> To be inclined not to the easiest,
> but to the most difficult;
> not to the most delightful, but to
> the hardest;
> When you turn toward something, you cease to
> cast yourself on the All. (Ascent I, 13, 6)

St. John challenges us to that struggle of asceticism that helps us achieve a true liberation and that generates an unselfish love. Applied to the life of an office worker or a housewife or a shopkeeper, Christian asceticism does not translate into the *Art of Positive Thinking*, but to embracing the Cross in all the pedestrian and routine circumstances - to see the force of love beyond all the adversities of life. There must be the conviction that we are able to do difficult things out of love. This flies in the face of so much hedonistic thinking of today: an attitude of rejection of the Cross that breeds so much mediocrity. It is only this willingness to accept the Cross that will allow one to live a moral life. And how difficult it is for people to live a moral life if priests, teachers, and theologians are telling people "that the teachings of the Church don't apply in their special circumstances!"

Christian asceticism applies in so many areas of our life: in social dealing with others (to avoid gossip and strive to overcome prejudices); in recreation and entertainment - use time for spiritual reading, study of our faith, avoidance of the kinds of TV shows and films that undermine Catholic values. [Malcom Muggeridge in his *Christ and the Media* states that the average person in his country spends 8 years (out of 60) watching TV].

What a responsibility we have to teach the truth. There can be no spirituality built on lies and moral confusion. For this reason, it is impossible to speak of spirituality without examining our attitude toward material goods. I often think of the episode in the Gospel where a young lad of deep religious sentiment and moral conduct approaches Jesus seeking spiritual fulfillment, and Jesus invites him to renunciation. He could not do it. He went away sad. His letters could have been epistles, he might have carried Christ's message to distant lands. Yet he rather walked into oblivion with his bank account intact.

Stewardship, Gospel attitude towards money is essential for any spirituality - especially in today's consumer society, a society where luxuries are labeled as necessities and Lazarus languishes on our doorstep. Our Catholic homes must look to the simplicity of Nazareth and not the artificial standards of Hollywood. How many young couples dupe themselves into not bringing life into the world in order to maintain a yuppie lifestyle?

The ecclesial dimension of the spirituality of lay Catholics is more important than ever. Our parishes must become centers of spirituality and evangelization. Mother Teresa was right when she stated that "the renewal of the Church will depend in great part on the renewal of priests." Renewal, therefore, requires priests who can be preachers, retreat masters, confessors, spiritual directors.

Catholic spirituality is never just "Jesus and me" - the ecclesial dimension must be present. Participation in the sacraments, liturgy, and parish life as well as such apostolic movements as the Third Order, Opus Dei, Cursillo (would there be any Spanish Catholics in New York without Cursillo?), Charismatic, Marriage Encounter, Focolare, and others areinvaluable in helping our Catholic people rediscover the interior life. I would ask the movements: help revitalize the parishes; reach beyond your communities.

Intimacy with God in the spiritual life should find an expression in involvement in the life of the Church. Pope Paul VI wrote in *Evangelii Nuntiandi*: "The evangelized person is an evangelizer." The interior life of our laity should induce them to become active in spreading the Kingdom, communicating Christ's truths, and transforming society by defending and promoting religious values in our schools, businesses, and places of recreation. It also implies giving witness to the faith of the Church when it is questioned, ridiculed, or trivialized. Part of the task of evangelization is to work for the poor and to promote the Church's social teachings, beginning with the Church's condemnation of abortion, which should be the centerpiece of Catholic social action in the United States.

The ecclesial dimension of our Catholic spirituality implies that as we strive for union with God, we strive at the same time to bring about union and reconciliation within the Church. Jesus' great prayer was for unity - "That all might be one, as we, Father, are one so that the world might believe." Jesus was praying for us. Moreover, when His disciples were fighting over the best places at the table, Jesus knelt down to wash their feet, to teach a lesson - that we must not fight for the first places at the table, but fight for the towel. Unity requires great patience, great capacity to forgive, great courage to defend, great loyalty to the Holy Father, and a great capacity for suffering. Unity requires preaching the work in season and out of season.

The unity of the Church has so many obstacles: on the one hand, consumerism, racism, xenophobia; on the other, dissidence, doctrinal confusion, and moral chaos. We cannot complacently allow the High Church/Low Church or American Church vs. Catholic Church syndrome to continue. We must be convinced that this goes directly against Jesus' explicit and most ardent desire that the unity among His disciples mirror that unity that exists in the Blessed Trinity.

There is much interest in spirituality today, but this interest will lead to an authentic renewal only if the Sacrament of Confession regains its rightful place in Catholic life. The confessional is the logical place for the Catholic lay person to begin the arduous pilgrimage to purification and illumination that leads to union with God. In this sacrament, the Church helps us to deepen our sense of morality and to overcome those loves that prevent us from reaching God's love. In this sacrament, we are called to conversion and to examine our behavior and attitudes in the light of the Gospel.

And it is in the confessional, in the solemn grace-filled moment of the sacrament, that the good confessor can clarify the teaching of the Church's magisterium and strengthen the resolve of the penitent to be faithful. For, indeed, the confessional has traditionally provided the masses of Catholics with the opportunity for spiritual direction and moral guidance without which authentic renewal is hardly possible. In the confessional, the Lord imparts the graces we need to grow in interior life, to glimpse His mercy, and to experience His healing love.

Somehow we must all do our best to get the word out - namely, that spirituality is what Catholicism is all about. Living the Pascal Mystery, proclaiming the Good News of Salvation is why we are here. Sometimes the sociological and political models of contemporary society obscure our vision of our mission and our purpose.

I would like to conclude by reading a passage from one of my favorite novels: Graham Greene's *The Power and the Glory*. In this scene, the "whiskey priest" is in prison - certain that he is about to be executed:

He felt only an immense disappointment because he had to go to God empty-handed, with nothing done at all. It seemed to him at that moment that it would have been quite easy to have been a saint. It would only have needed a little self-restraint and a little courage. He felt like someone who has missed happiness by seconds at an appointed place. He knew now that in the end there was only one thing that counted - to be a saint.

Spiritual Renewal and Social Reform
Liberation Theology
by
Brian Benestad

The Sacred Congregation for the Doctrine of the Faith has issued two documents on the same subject in less than one year. They are the "Instruction on Certain Aspects of the Theology of Liberation" (6 August 1985)[1] and the "Instruction on Christian Freedom and Liberation" (22 March 1986)[2]. The first "Instruction" focuses on deviations characteristic of certain forms of liberation theology; the second, while not claiming to be exhaustive, presents a positive vision of Christian freedom and liberation. It also effectively promotes the common good of society, especially the interests of the poor and the oppressed, and, at the same time, shows how to preserve Catholicism from losing its soul while working for justice and peace. Contrary to reports in the media, the second "Instruction" does not water down assertions made in the first. A number of the same themes are found in both documents -- spiritual conversion as a priority over change of structures, sin as an evil greater than poverty and oppression, freedom from sin as the most radical liberation, the social effects of personal sin, love as the supreme rule of social life, the obligation of all to promote the common good, opposition to class struggle, and the openness and limits of Catholic social teaching. The two documents form a unity and must be read together. My comments are limited to a summary of the second "Instruction."

The first chapter summarizes the advantages and disadvantages of the modern liberation process. As advantages, it mentions the abolition of legal slavery, development of human rights doctrines, the promotion of equality and fraternity, access to culture for greater numbers of people, and the opportunity in many countries for citizens to participate in political and social life.

The Sacred Congregation for the Doctrine of the Faith goes into more detail regarding the disadvantages of the modern liberation movement, concluding that the movement remains ambiguous with "threats of deadly forms of bondage." The Congregation asks whether technology can be prevented from becoming an oppressive power and from enslaving future generations. It characterizes as major errors certain Enlightenment beliefs, viz., that progress in science, technology, and economics necessarily promote freedom and that the goal of the self-sufficient individual "is the satisfaction of his own interest in the enjoyment of earthly goods." It also mentions the widespread self-destruction caused by the young seeking liberation in drugs. Lastly, it points out that the modern exultation of autonomy has led some to regard all morality as an "irrational limit" and many more to regard belief in God as an obstacle to human freedom.

Chapter Two explains the Christian understanding of freedom and sin. Christian liberation is primarily freedom from sin and the power of death, accomplished by the death and resurrection of Jesus Christ. Sin and death are the greatest evils, greater than poverty and oppression. The redemption wrought by Jesus is, therefore, the most radical liberation. Christian liberation is also freedom for goodness. The good is the goal of freedom. In consequence, man becomes free to the extent that he comes to a knowledge of the truth and to the extent that this truth -- and not any other force -- guides his will.[3] Christian liberation, then, depends on maintaining the link between truth, goodness, and freedom. There can be no freedom unless the human person can come to a knowledge of the good.

Sin is contempt for God and disordered love of self. Sin is the practical rejection of the truth about human existence. By sinning, people lie to themselves and deny realtiy that stares them in the face. Through sin, "man rejects the truth and places his own will above it." In not harmonizing "his will with his nature," a person engages in self-destructive behaviour.

Disorders in the human heart, brought about by sin, inevitably cause disorders in the family and in all society. The root cause of unjust structures is personal sin. Sin "is the radical reason for the tragedies which mark the history of freedom." The connection between sin and societal injustices has been a major theme of John Paul II.

Chapter Three explains the relation of freedom and love in the Hebrew Scriptures and the New Testament. The Exodus of the Israelites from Egypt cannot be understood simply as a political fact. Its more profound meaning is religious. "God sets his people free and gives them descendants, a land and a law but within a covenant." The central message about freedom of the New Testament is that "grace frees us from sin and places us in communion with God." Christ's death and resurrection make possible the liberation from sin and the justification by grace which is received through faith and the Church's sacraments.

The mission of the Church, discussed in Chapter Four, is to foster liberation by means of evangelization. Through the word of God and the sacraments, the Church frees people from sin and leads them into communion with one another and with God. The Church has no specific mission in the political, economic or social order. Nevertheless, carrying out her proper mission, the Church has a profound effect on the social order. Accepting the mysterious plan of salvation has "liberating effects upon individual and social existence." If the Church's members accept the universal call to holiness, "they will bring forth fruits of justice and peace in their families and in the places where they work and live." An evangelized laity will bring the leaven of the Gospel to bear on every earthly reality. It is also part of the vocation of the laity to do what is not appropriate for pastors of the Church -- "to intervene directly in the political construction and organization of social life." The Church is also faithful to her mission of condemning evils in society, whether they take the form of law, customs or political movements.

It is part of the mission of the Church, in addition, to show a love for the poor. She sees all poverty as "an evil from which human beings must be freed as completely as possible." The causes of poverty, according to the "Instruction," are sin and human frailty, including ignorance regarding the elements of sound social order. The Church's "love of preference" for the poor encompasses those in a "situation of poverty, scorn, rejection, or powerlessness," including unborn children killed by abortion, the abandoned elderly or anyone rejected spiritually or physically by society. The option for the poor is not a partisan choice expressed by "reductive sociological and ideological categories." The Church rather shows love for the poor through her own works of charity and through the communication of her social doctrine. The latter attempts to promote the common good by elaborating political principles and fostering virtue as well as structural changes in society.

As for the basic communities and other Christian groups that have emerged in response to the "cry of the poor," they are a source of great hope for the Church, if their members accept the whole Christian faith, including the hierarchy, the sacraments, and the teaching of the magisterium.

The last chapter of the "Instruction" contains a brief overview of the social doctrine of the Church. The central affirmation of that doctrine is the "permanent need" for conversion and the formation of character, along with the practice of virtue in the quest for a just social order. Conversion of heart must take precedence over structural changes:

> The priority given to structures and technical organizations over the person and the requirements of his dignity is the expression of a materialistic anthropology and is contrary to the construction of a just social order.[4]

This has been a perennial theme of Catholic political wisdom going all the way back to the Church Fathers. In the last twenty years or so, the understanding of a just social order grounded in virtue has been obscured in the minds of many, including bishops, priests, and theologians. In his recent interview on the state of the Church, Cardinal Ratzinger remarked:

> It is also painful to be confronted with the illusion, so essentially unChristian which is present among priests and theologians that a new man and a new world can be created, not by calling each

individual to conversion, but only by changing the social and economic structures. For it is precisely personal sin that is in reality at the root of unjust social structures. Those who really desire a more human society need to begin with the root, not with the trunk and branches, of the tree of injustice. The issue here is one of fundamental Christian truths, yet they are depricatingly dismissed as "alienating" and "spiritualistic."[5]

While moral integrity in leaders and citizens is a necessary condition for the health of any society, it is not yet sufficient. The "Instruction" adds that members of society need to acquire essential technical and scientific skills, as well as knowledge of sound political principles and "education in the political prudence needed for guiding and running human affairs." It is especially the role of the laity to work in a prudent manner for the change of unjust structures.

The social doctrine of the Church does not advocate any particular social, economic or political system, but offers "a set of principles for reflection and criteria for judgement and also directives for action." It is not based solely on revelation and tradition but also on the resources of human wisdom and all the sciences. Consequently, this doctrine will contain both permanently valid principles and contingent judgments. In other words, Catholic social teaching can change in a way that Catholic teaching on faith and morals cannot.

The foundation of Catholic social teaching is the dignity of the human person who is created in the image of God. The human person is by nature social and has natural rights and duties. Intimately linked to the dignity of the human person are the principles of solidarity and subsidiarity. According to the principle of solidarity, all people have an obligation "to contribute to the common good of society at all its levels." Because of this principle, Church doctrine opposes all forms of political and social individualism. According to the principle of subsidiarity, "Neither the state nor any society must ever substitute itself for the initiative and responsibility of individuals and inter-mediate communities at the level on which they can function, nor must they take away the room for their freedom." It places the Church in opposition to all forms of collectivism. Subsidiarity requires participation and community at all levels of society. It really insures that everyone will have an opportunity to be personally responsible for various aspects of the common good. These two principles help people make judgements about social situations, structures, and systems.

While the "Instruction" points out that all have an obligation to promote the common good, it mentions that certain classes have special responsibility. Intellectuals, for example, have moral and political responsibility to help oppose tyrants who impose ideologies "contrary to the culture of the people." The "Instruction" also criticizes culpable passivity in democratic leaders who fail to protect the constitutional rights of large numbers of men and women.

The "Instruction" does not attempt to give a complete description of the common good, but does offer some indication as to its meaning under the rubric of the "civilization of love." Progress towards that goal requires ambitious programs to liberate millions of people from poverty and tyranny. Action must begin with a prodigious effort in education: "education for the civilization of work, education for solidarity, access to culture for all."

Echoing *Laborem exercens*, the Congregation's document describes work as the key to the whole social question. "The solution of most of the serious problems related to poverty is to be found in the formation of a true civilization of work."[6] Work is seen as a very important means of fostering liberation. While the "Instruction" repeats a number of themes from *Laborem exercens*, it does not discuss in any detail what would be necessary to promote a civilization of work, e.g., healthy families and a sound educational system.

As for education to solidarity, the "Instruction" lays emphasis on creating new structures of solidarity, e.g., between the richer nations and those still developing.

The remarks on culture are less sparse than those on solidarity, yet they do not go into any great detail. To ensure access to culture, every human being needs the opportunity to develop intellectual capacities and other talents, moral virtue, and the ability to relate to others. The family is primarily responsible for providing this kind of education; the state should guarantee, promote and supplement the role of the family. The latter, of course, will make use of schools, private or public to fulfill its responsibilities. The state should provide financial aid to private schools which provide assistance to families.

Conclusion

The second "Instruction" clearly gives no support for the aberrations of certain liberation theologians. It discourages the political re-reading of Scripture, easy recourse to violence, the reduction of Christianity to a this-worldly project and the attempt to create a "new man" and a "new society" by simply changing economic and political structures. Furthermore, it gives no encouragement to the tendency of the U.S. episcopal conference to pursue justice by laying stress on the formulation of policy proposals. On the contrary, it stresses that the pastors of the Church should not "intervene directly in the political construction and organization of social life." Rather, pastors should concentrate on evangelizing and communicating the Catholic social doctrine.

Finally, the second "Instruction" does reiterate the long standing Church teaching about the legitimacy of recourse to armed struggle as a last resort in the struggle against "an obvious and prolonged tyranny." The media focused on this statement and helped create the false impression that this "Instruction" made important concessions to the liberation theologies criticized in the first "Instruction." In reality, this second "Instruction," a balanced and moving document, is a very nice restatement of things said by John Paul II and Cardinal Ratzinger on other occasions. Of special import is the way it both preserves the integrity of Catholicism and shows how Catholic teaching brings immeasurable benefits to the political and social order.

Footnotes:

1. See *Origins*, 14 (1984): 193-204.

2. *Ibid.*, 15 (1986): 713-728.

3. *Ibid.*, p. 718, item #26.

4. *Ibid.*, p. 724, item #75.

5. *Ratzinger Report* (San Francisco: Ignatius Press, 1980), p. 190.

6. *Origins*, 15 (1986): 725, item #83.

"Liberation Theology"
by
John Gueguen

It is well that we are opening our conference with reflections on the Instruction on Christian Freedom and Liberation. *The Religion and Society Report* for June, 1986 called it "the most impressive and potentially significant statement on theology and politics to have emerged from any official church source in many years. No responsible discussion of these questions can bypass it. No serious discussant should want to."

Professor Benestad has very well summarized the Instruction, laying emphasis upon its concluding section -- the need for a thorough education in the social doctrine of the Church. With this summary before us, there is no need for me to extend it, although I mean to call attention to certain points that seem to me especially important. Beyond that, I may be permitted, I hope, to develop an interpretive analysis so as to suggest a focus for our discussion.

Professor Benestad noted that the 1986 Instruction presents a more positive vision of Christian liberation than the 1984 critique of recent liberation movements which lack that proper theological orientation. In my view it does even more; it proclaims with confidence the victory of the ancient Christian message over attempts by dissident theologians to alter that message in favor of revolutionary ideologies which pursue a purely earthly salvation. We read: "A new phase in the history of freedom is opening before us" (sec. 24).

Beyond the natural development of the theme Cardinal Ratzinger's Congregation embarked upon in 1984, could there be a further explanation for this dramatic shift in tone between the two documents? A clue is provided: that joyful outcry of Mary when she visited Elizabeth in the second mystery of the Rosary. I quote: "Thus a theology of freedom and liberation which faithfully echoes Mary's Magnificat *preserved in the Church's memory* is something needed by the times in which we live" (sec. 98; my emphasis). Note especially the words, "preserved in the Church's memory." Between 1984 and 1986 the Church has had occasion to remember something. Perhaps the Extraordinary Synod of 1985, four months before the second Instruction was published, was the occasion for this exercise in recollection (anamnesis) of Vatican II.

The Council is expressly mentioned toward the close of the Instruction (sec. 96) as a source of illumination in the task of proclaiming the Gospel truthfully in our time -- a task to which the Church, we are told, wishes to devote all of her energies so as to evoke an immense liberating effort.

In any case, following Mary's precedent, the Sacred Congregation is led to meditate on her prayer and finding it a most fruitful meditation, warmly commends it to theologians concerned with the social question in general and with poverty in particular. It is this meditation on Mary's faithfulness, we are told, that can prevent derailment into false notions of liberation and begin to repair the damage they have already done.

What do we find in the Magnificat that is so stimulating to the memory of the Church? Two things.

First, the theological virtues: The Sacred Congregation finds in Mary's prayer the virtue of faith so needed in the present atmosphere of rebellion and infidelity. Mary affirms simply and straightforwardly her knowledge of the plan of salvation devised by God, and her firm allegiance to it. By meditation on the Magnificat we can discover the potent liberating effects of faith for persons and for societies (sec. 97).

Going on to the virtue of hope, the Congregation finds in Mary's prayer the confident expectation of eternal happiness, the greatest imaginable freedom -- an expectation which we are to nourish likewise as we make our way through the inevitably disordered passage of this world. (sec. 59).

And the Congregation finds in Mary's prayer the perfection of love in charity, especially in the way she anticipates the New Commandment and the fullness of a Christian praxis which it contains (sec. 71, 55).

The meditation on the Magnificat which the Instruction recommends enables us to distinguish Christian faith from the cynical manipulation of science by modern ideologists who try to advance a thoroughly secularized notion of knowledge. The meditation on the Magnificat enables us to distinguish Christian hope from placement of all confidence in temporal progress and the groundless expectation of an earthly utopia. And this meditation saves the Christian virtue of charity from perversion by hatred and violence ostensibly undertaken as the expression of a love for the poor which is deprived of supernatural vision (sec. 76, 77).

In view of all this, I would suggest a more positive rephrasing of Professor Benestad's opening assertion that the Instruction shows how to preserve Catholicism from losing its soul in the work for justice and peace. I suggest, rather, that the Instruction shows us how to work for justice and peace by recalling why and how the soul of Catholicism *is* saved. This is the lesson of the Magnificat. Temporal justice and peace are certainly good aspirations, but they are to be obtained above all through the cultivation of the theological virtues:

> There is no gap between love of neighbor and desire for justice (sec. 57);

Hope does not weaken commitment to the progress of the earthly city (sec. 60);

It is really in the light of faith that one comes to understand how salvation history is the history of liberation from evil and of the introduction of humanity into the true freedom of the children of God (sec. 97).

Thus, the Ratzinger Congregation concludes, Mary is the most perfect image of freedom and of liberation. Ironically, this appears to be most appreciated by the poor, the very ones who have been instrumentalized by preachers of violent class struggle and revolution. It is the poor who flock to Guadalupe, Lourdes, and Fatima to get closer to their mother, for she remnds them that the mercy of the Lord endures forever, that the strength available to us in this life is a divine loan which we can never pay back. It is the poor who understand -- instinctively, as it were -- that Mary leads to Christ, who alone accomplishes their liberation and is the way to freedom (sec. 22). The learned who want to help the poor have, themselves, much to learn *from* the poor (as Pastor Neuhaus also observed in his commentary on the Instruction in the *Religion and Society Report*).

We come now to the second way in which the Church's memory is stimulated by the Magnificat: Besides an appreciation of our need for the theological virtues, especially in the present world context, the meditation on the Magnificat also clarifies brilliantly the true meaning of these concepts, liberation and freedom, and the relationship of the two.

Liberation is deliverance *from* -- from evil in its most radical form, which is to say, from sin, and from death, the consequence of sin. As Mary shows, this liberation is mankind's fundamental aspiration after the fall from grace (sec. 23, 5).

Freedom, on the other hand, is the capacity *for* -- for good in its most radical form, which is to say, for virtue, and for the happy life to which it is ordained. The heart of Christian freedom is the grace which enables us to advance in the supernatural virtues (sec. 26, 52).

Liberation prepares the way for freedom, i.e., in the primary instance salvific liberation from sin through the passion and death of Christ. And then, with this context firmly established, we can think correctly about pursuing temporal liberation through scientific and technological development and through social and political structures (sec. 31, 71).

Unless we first realize that we *are* in bondage to sin and therefore stand in need to be liberated from *it*, we are likely to exaggerate and misunderstand the various forms of temporal bondage which have afflicted and ever will afflict us on account of the natural limitations of our human condition and the inheritance of sin to which we daily contribute. Unless we strive for awareness of the profound disturbance of the order that is proper to our being, the Instruction suggests, we are bound to make mistakes in apprehending the various forms of disorder that meet us in the world. For (as Professor Benestad pointed out) such disorders are rooted in the disorder of sin, in the *contemptus Dei* which leads to *conversio ad creaturam* -- the radical abuse of freedom in disordered self-love and a disordered love of others (sec. 37, 41).

Seen in this light, temporal misery is perceived to be a sign of our need for salvation even as we strive to relieve it by all available means -- even (as Professor Benestad mentioned) armed resistance to tyranny, if it should come to that as a last resort (sec. 79).

Having thus meditated on the Magnificat and therein discovered the truth about liberation and freedom, the Instruction can then place in proper perspective two other Biblical passages which have been misinterpreted by the secularizing theologians of liberation. These passages are the Exodus episode from the Old Testament (sec. 44-46) and the Sermon on the Mount from the New Testament -- which is the completion and the fullness of the Exodus in the transcendence of the Kingdom of God; that is, the freedom that follows liberation (sec. 62, 63).

To conclude: Pope John Paul II, in a new crusade to liberate the old countries of the West from neopaganism, has said that our times call for the active presence of saints; as the original evangelization was accomplished by saints, so must this new evangelization be accomplished by saints. Here, I think, is the ultimate reason for the confident tone of the Instruction on Freedom and Liberation. The Church has not lost her capacity to rouse aspirations to sanctity through the true poverty which is liberation from those things that stand between us and Christ and through the true wealth which is free devotion to those in need, seeing Christ in them. In a recent conversation in Chicago, Mother Teresa summed up this condition for sanctity as freedom of the heart.

The holy men and women who are to restore the Christian orientation of society by healing the tragic separation between the Gospel and culture will learn, as all the saints did, to derive inspiration and support from Mary, the first one to be liberated from sin and therefore the one whom all generations call blessed -- that is, truly free (sec. 96, 57, 70).

These new saints will especially need to be drawn, the Instruction concludes, from the ranks of the laity who are well instructed in the social doctrine of the Church and capable of providing leadership in the sanctification of all walks of life, especially (as Professor Benestad stressed) through their professional work. I close with several lines from Cardinal Ratzinger's Instruction which speak urgently to this need:

To intervene directly in the political construction and organization of social life.... forms part of the vocation of the laity acting on their own initiative with their fellow citizens.... The work of salvation is thus seen to be indissolubly linked to the task of improving and raising the conditions of human life in this world (sec. 80).

The Bishops' U.S. Economic Pastoral
by
Carl A. Anderson*

I appreciate the invitation to offer you some reflections on the subject of "Spiritual Renewal and the Reform of Social Institutions" with particular reference to the Third Draft of the bishops' pastoral on economics. This is especially the case following the substantial review of the Second Draft by Regis Factor before an earlier meeting of the Fellowship. I will not try to add to the marvelous contribution Professor Factor has already made to the understanding of the document through his analysis of the Church's social teachings. Rather, I intend to consider the Third Draft from the standpoint of what the document contributes to the efforts of those of us in the public policy area whose day to day work confronts questions of poverty, employment and welfare policies.

I offer these observations on my own behalf and not as a response by the Administration to the bishops' document. I think a very convincing argument can be made against any government -- but especially our government -- from officially commenting upon a "pastoral" letter. But when any group of citizens proposes specific policy and programmatic changes in governmental programs, it is entirely appropriate for those of us with experience in the development and management of these programs to share that experience.

In light of the creative analysis of social and economic problems provided by John Paul II in *Laborem Exercens* and *Familiaris Consortio*, many looked forward to the development by the National Conference of Bishops of a pastoral letter on Catholic social teaching and the United States economy. But whereas a reader of the Third Draft of the American bishops' economic pastoral might have expected to find an analysis building upon the earlier work of the Holy Father, this, unfortunately, is not the case. The bishops have contributed to the sense of national urgency in regard to the plight of the poor. But the Third Draft's repeated incantation of a preferential option for the poor as the criterion of a morally sound economy is no substitute for a straightforward analysis of existing governmental policies intended to implement such a preferential option.

Early on in the pastoral letter, the writers of the Third Draft set a high goal for themselves. They state: "The economic challenge of today has many parallels with the political challenge that confronted the founders of our nation. In order to create a new form of political democracy they were compelled to develop ways of thinking and political institutions that had never existed before... We believe the time has come for a similar experiment in securing economic rights: the creation of an order that guarantees the minimum conditions of human dignity in the economic sphere for every person."[1]

This is a lofty challenge indeed, and one which the serious student of social policy will find unmet in the Third Draft of *Economic Justice For All.* This is not only because the Third Draft contains errors; more importantly, it ignores much of the social science evidence which has accumlated over the past decade. This failure weakens the ability of the draft to offer us very much that is new in our approach to these problems.

While I do not wish to spend much time on technical problems or misleading statements in the document, I will offer three examples. First, in its discussion of the right of private property (a discussion which takes up approximately 20 lines in the document) the authors observe: " 'Private property does not constitute for anyone an absolute or unconditioned right. No one is justified in keeping for his exclusive use what he does not need, when others lack necessities' ... For example; these limits are the basis of society's exercise of eminent domain over privately owned land needed for roads or other essential public goods."[2]

Now what needs to be said about this is that society's exercise of eminent domain has nothing to do with one's moral or legal right to one's property. After all, when the State condemns my house in order to build a highway, it is not taking from me what I do not need in order to give it to someone in more need than I. Neither does the State argue that my right to this property is not absoute, since when it does take my home it expressly recognizes my right to it through the constitutional requirement of just compensation. To compare the Church's teaching in this area with notions of eminent domain is simply misleading at best.

A second example can be found in the document's discussion of the causes of poverty among women. A primary cause of this problem according to the authors of the Third Draft is wage discrimination against women and the fact that "Women who work outside their homes full-time and year-round earn only 61 percent of what men earn. Thus, being employed full-time is not by itself a remedy for poverty among women."[3] You will notice that the wage comparison being made here is not one between men and women of equivalent education, age, and work experience. Should such factors be included, we might be surprised to find that in some occupations women's earnings equal or even surpass those of men. Neither are we told whether earning only 61 percent of what men earn still places one above the poverty line. But then the draft fails to cite any authority for either of its observations.

A third example can be found in the document's assertion that public assistance programs should provide recipients with adequate levels of support. As evidence that current programs do not do so, the document states: "At present only 4 percent of poor families with children receive enough cash welfare benefits to lift them out of poverty."[4] But what the document fails to mention is that cash benefits are only one part of a combined benefit package which contain substantial non-cash assistance. To exclude the value of non-cash benefits, such as Medicaid, housing, food stamps, school lunches, and legal services, as the Third Draft does, is to seriously misrepresent the level of available benefits to the poor. In 1984, for example, if the actual poverty rate had been adjusted for the market value of non-cash benefits, the poverty rate would have fallen from 14.4 percent to 9.7 percent.[5]

More important, however, than these difficulties is that a fundamental premise of the Third Draft is not only misleading, but from a public policy perspective almost unintelligible. The document states: "Recent Catholic social thought regards the task of overcoming... patterns of exclusion and powerlessness as a most basic demand of justice. Stated positively, justice demands that social institutions be ordered in a way that guarantees all persons the ability to participate actively in the economic, political and cultural life of society."[6] Shortly thereafter, the writers reach this startling conclusion: "The first step in such an effort is the development of a new cultural consensus that the basic economic conditions of human welfare are essential to human dignity and are due persons by right."[7]

The difficulty with this premise is that there already exists a firm social, cultural and political consensus in American society that the basic economic conditions of human welfare be met. To suggest otherwise, as the Third Draft does, simply does not compute. The social policy issues confronting decision-makers in 1986 are not the same as those confronting decision-makers at the beginning of the War on Poverty in the mid-1960s.

Last year government expenditures on income transfer programs at the federal level alone amounted to approximately $377.1 billion.[8] That figure represents an astonishing increase in the national commitment to social benefit programs. Since 1960, we have experienced nearly a complete reversal between the federal government's commitment to national defense and its commitment to payments to individuals. In 1960, defense spending as a percentage of the Gross National Product amounted to 9.7 percent while federal spending on payments for individuals amounted to only 4.9 percent. By 1984, the figures had nearly reversed with defense spending totaling only 5.9 percent of GNP while payments to individuals had increased to 11 percent.[9] During the last 10 to 15 years specific benefit programs have made even more dramatic increases; for example, more than 16,000 percent in the case of food stamps and more than 500 percent in the case of Medicaid and Medicare.[10]

The fundamental social policy issue of the 1980's is not whether we can create a new cultural consensus to aid the poor among us, but how successful we have been in the past and how successful we may be in the future in implementing the already existing consensus to improve the economic life of poor Americans. The political economy of the United States is already well down the path of distributive justice in principle. The question which now needs to be asked -- and which is not really asked in a meaningful way in the Third Draft -- is the extent to which the present government income transfer programs actually succeed in implementing the demands of distributive justice.

In the time that I have remaining, I would like to address this issue. In doing so, I call your attention to a forthcoming study of the Joint Economic Committee of Congress by Professors Lowell Gallaway and Richard Vedder of Ohio University. Their study entitled, *Poverty, Income Distribution, the Family and Public Policy*,[11] builds upon those of many others before them and is particularly important in our context because Gallaway and Vedder address many issues directly related to problems discussed in the Third Draft. In their study, Gallaway and Vedder seek to understand the relationship between welfare benefits and incidence of poverty, unemployment, and child rearing, not to mention abortion and illegitimacy. The failure of the Third Draft to come to grips with evidence such as that presented by Professors Gallaway, Vedder, and many of their colleagues -- and most importantly, the failure of the Third Draft to even ask the same questions -- threatens the document's relevancy to present social policy discussions.

While the Third Draft argues for an increase in cash payments for welfare recipients, it ignores the more fundamental issue of the relationship between direct income transfer programs and the reduction of poverty. An analysis of this question undertaken by Sheldon Danziger and Robert Plotnick[12] found that $12.6 billion (in 1983 dollars) of cash transfer payments in 1967 reduced poverty 0.7 percentage points. By 1974, such cash transfer payments had risen to $26.6 billion (again in 1983 dollars) but had resulted in only a 1.0 percentage reduction. Thus, from zero to $12.6 billion in cash payments, the marginal reduction in the poverty rate per billion dollars of transfers was .056. But from $12.6 billion to $26.6 billion in transfers the marginal reduction in the poverty rate was only a surprising .021 percentage points per billion of transfers. The Danziger and Plotnick research strongly suggests that while a certain level of cash benefits is beneficial in reducing poverty, increasing benefits may not increase the rate of poverty reduction.

This decreasing marginal rate of poverty reduction suggests the existence of a threshold of cash benefits beyond which additional transfer payments may actually increase the poverty rate rather than decrease it. Reviewing the Danziger-Plotnick findings, Gallaway and Vedder suggest "that the marginal rate of poverty reduction may actually have become negative at 1974 levels of cash transfers."[13] In other words, giving more money keeps more people poor. Danziger and Plotnick observe that cash payments have reached such proportions that the accompanying work disincentive effects actually lead to higher rates of official poverty.

The Danziger-Plotnick thesis is consistent with the earlier Seattle-Denver Income Maintenance Experiments in which poor families in both cities were studied over a ten-year period with control groups in both cities given a cash benefit of 115 percent of the poverty line. The study found that for every $100 provided to male-headed families, earnings fell by $25 to $50 and that for female-headed families the effect was even greater.[14]

The concept proposed by Gallaway and Vedder of a Poverty-Welfare Curve, in which crossing a threshold of increasing welfare benefits effects an increase in poverty, is consistent with the behavior of the poverty rate in recent years. From the inception of the War on Poverty in the 1960's through 1973, the poverty rate in the United States consistently declined until it reached 11.1 percent. Since that time it has just as consistently increased until it reached a post-1965 high of 15.3 percent in 1983.

This Poverty-Welfare Curve is also consistent with the increase in child poverty. While the poverty rate for children generally exceeds the overall rate, the relationship between those two rates has shifted dramatically during the last three decades. In 1959, for example, the child poverty rate was 4.5 percentage points greater than the aggregate rate. By 1969, that difference had fallen to only 1.7 percent. By the next year, however, that trend had reversed and continued to widen until it stood at 6.6 percentage points in 1984.[15]

Certainly a number of factors produced this reversal. One factor, no doubt, was the 1968 decision of the United States Supreme Court to strike down the welfare eligibility requirement of many States which prohibited a "substitute father" from being present in the home of an unmarried welfare mother.[16] By allowing cash benefits to unmarried mothers under the Aid to Families with Dependent Children program in households in which a "substitute father" was present, the Supreme Court redirected America's welfare program to provide a substantial incentive for the creation of non-traditional families.

Another factor too was the decision of 49 states during this time period to institute some form of no-fault divorce. While these statutory changes were defended on the basis of sexual equality, the economic consequences of no-fault divorce are now understood to affect the spouses differently. Following a ten-year study of no-fault divorce, sociologist Lenore Weitzman of Stanford University found that the impoverishment of women and children is too often a result of the new statutory scheme. Her research shows that on the average, divorced women and their children experience a 73 percent decrease in their standard of living following divorce while their former husbands experience a 42 percent rise in their living standard.[17]

The Bureau of the Census indicates that families headed by never-married and formerly-married women account for 47 percent of the 7.6 million families with incomes below the poverty level. Research cited by the United States Civil Rights Commission in its 1983 report entitled, *A Growing Crisis: Disadvantaged Women and Their Children,* suggests that the increasing incidence of marital disruption and the extraordinary rise in unwed motherhood "are responsible for essentially all of the growth in poverty since 1970... and that they show no signs of abating as the unwed birth and divorce rates continue to climb rapidly."[18]

These trends have proven devastating to millions of America's children when coupled with the substantial work disincentives accompanying the present delivery of welfare benefits. The Danziger-Plotnick and Gallaway-Vedder studies as well as the Seattle-Denver Income Maintenance Experiments demonstrate the substantial work disincentives of increasing cash benefits to female-headed households.

In the Third Draft, the disproportion of female versus male-headed households in poverty is attributed in large measure to wage discrimination, insufficient affirmative action programs and a failure to provide pay equity for jobs traditionally held by women. Yet, these explanations fail to explain why it is that so many non-poor women and especially non-poor mothers of small children work when so many poor women do not. In 1983, among women with children under the age of six years, 65.8 percent of poor women did not work, while only 32 percent -- less than half that other figure -- of non-poor women did not work. This disparity between poor and non-poor mothers is not simply the result of jobs not being available for poor women who wanted to find work but could not. Of those poor mothers with children under six who did not work, 50.4 percent stated they did not in order to "keep house." Indeed, in 1984, only 7.2 percent of poor mothers who were also the head of their households worked full time. Gallaway and Vedder conclude: "Poor mothers in similar child rearing circumstances show a greater tendency to refrain from working than do non-poor mothers."[19]

One explanation of this disparity not considered by the Third Draft is the relationship between the amount of cash benefits to poor mothers, the cost of raising children and the increase in the number of children in poverty. Drawing on data from the late 1970's, Gallaway and Vedder find two important conclusions: first, that until a poverty child reaches the age of 12, welfare benefits actually exceed the marginal costs of raising the child; and, second, by the time the child reaches the age of 17 years, those benefits will exceed the cost of raising him by $3,000.[20] Gallaway and Vedder have developed a statistical model which finds that had welfare payments remained at the 1969 level, the povety rate among children in 1984 would have been 3.9 percent lower than actually reported. According to their findings, "...it appears that poverty among children was over twenty percent greater than it would have been in the absence of the massive post-1969 growth in the number and size of federal programs."[21] If correct, that translates into 2.5 million more children in poverty because of increases in public assistance.

This conclusion is supported by the trends regarding the increase state by state in child poverty when related to the differing benefit levels of the states. Between 1969 and 1979, the fifteen states with the highest cash benefit levels experienced a 26.1 percent increase in child poverty while the fifteen states with the lowest levels of AFDC payments experienced an average *decrease* in child poverty of 14.9 percent. This difference in trends remains even after controlling for differing economic conditions among the states.

If an increased level of cash benefits contributes to the growth of children in poverty, one may ask whether it also contributes to the growth of female headed-households in which no husband is present. Gallaway and Vedder answer that such an association exists there too. Their statistical analysis (which factored in variables which might affect the composition of households such as war and unemployment) found that the rise in cash benefit payments alone was associated with a 4.7 percent increase, by 1981, in the proportion of households without a father present. In other words, increased benefits were associated with the creation of more than 2.8 million families without a husband present affecting approximately 10 million women and children. While including variables for race, urbanization and a three year time lag between benefit level change and family composition, this analysis suggest that if a high benefit state, such as New York, had in 1977 adopted the AFDC benefit level of a low benefit state like Texas, by 1980, New York would have had 159,000 fewer female-headed families in poverty.[22]

These findings are also consistent with the results of the earlier Seattle-Denver Income Maintenance Experiments which found a significant rise in the level of marriage dissolution associated with cash payments to intact families. Such large payments, in this case amounting to 115 percent of the poverty level, substantially undercut the husband's economic role within the family. The trap for intact families which such payments create is that, although the benefits are initially provided while the husband is present, benefit payments will continue to the wife and children following divorce. In addition, the economies of scale within marriage may be compensated for upon divorce by other government benefits related to housing, food, health care, and energy costs. Thus, it would appear that the same economic incentives accompanying large cash benefits which affect a woman's decision to begin a family outside marriage may also influence her decision to discontinue a marriage. These economic incentives appear to be heightened by the judicial decision to permit benefits to continue in spite of the presence of a "substitute father" in the home to whom the woman is not married.

Gallaway and Vedder also find that "the divorce impact of rising federal public aid has been very substantial" and "that generous outlays of public assistance to help lower-income Americans has contributed to marital instability and dissolution."[23] They calculate that every billion dollars (in 1980 dollars) of public aid creates approximately eight thousand divorces annually.

This evidence argues against the recommendations of the Third Draft that the federal government should raise benefits to the poor by establishing a national minimum benefit level in cash assistance programs and that benefits under the Aid to Families with Dependent Children program be mandated for two-parent families.[24] In light of the recent findings we have been discussing, the implementation of these recommendations may be the surest way to plunge millions of women and children into poverty. A more productive recommendation, however, is the Third Draft's incorporation of the concept --implemented in recent comprehensive tax reform legislation -- that families with incomes below the poverty level not be required to pay federal income tax.[25] As George Gilder recently observed in the pages of *Catholicism in Crisis*, the United States today "faces a tragic crisis of government supported family decay."[6] Removing unfair tax burdens on America's families is one sure way of beginning to repair that decay. The Third Draft should go further in exploring the full meaning of tax fairness for families.

Historically, the family has proven to be the best intergenerational vehicle for the climb out of poverty by millions of Americans. The cadences of our social life by which infancy becomes youth, youth merges into maturity, and maturity ripens into old age are essentially familial processes. When government steps in to substitute its activity for that of the family, it often becomes a very poor substitute indeed. This is not only because of the unintended consequences which often accompany government programs -- some of which we have discussed today, but also because government has done a poor job in targeting those people to be helped. In 1983, for example, 49.4 percent of households receiving at least one of the four major non-cash benefits were above the poverty line. In 1984, 35 percent of households with incomes over the poverty level received cash benefits.[27] Not only may such misdirection of assistance deprive those Americans living under the poverty threshold of needed assistance, but it also undermines public confidence and support for these programs.

I would like to conclude my remarks with a slightly longer quotation from the conclusion of Gilder's article: "... I believe in all the essentials of Catholic teaching on sex and family. I arrived at these beliefs through laborious research in the secular literature on the subject and through long experience and observation of families rich and poor, all at a time when I regarded the Catholic Church as a retrograde body and myself as some kind of agnostic. I now believe in the divine inspiration of these Catholic insights and contend that a society can defy them only at the cost of an increasing estrangement from God. If (someone) sincerely wants a family policy, he should merely support measures that make it possible for Catholics and others to follow Catholic moral codes without dooming their families to poverty and turmoil. Most Catholics have long suffered a deep conflict between the teaching of their church and the dictates of current national economic and social policy. Any Catholic politician should resolve to eliminate that conflict. In purely secular terms, the Catholic view of sex and family has been entirely vindicated by recent events."[28]

Finally, Gilder reminds us that, "The fundamental fact of families is that... you must be committed -- to a sacred and sacrificial ideal that perpetuates and redeems human life," And that insight, I would suggest to you, is the beginning of spiritual renewal and the reform of social institutions.

* Special Assistant to the President of the United States. The views expressed are those of the author and are not those of the Executive Office of the President.

1. National Conference of Catholic Bishops, Economic Justice For All (Third Draft, 1986) p. 27.

2. *Id.*, p. 32.

3. *Id.*, pp. 48-49.

4. *Id.*, p. 56.

5. Source: United States Bureau of the Census, Current Population Reports, Series P-60.

6. *Supra* note 1 at p. 22.

7. *Id.*, p. 23.

8. Source: Executive Office of the President, Budget of the United States Government, 1987.

9. Source: Executive Office of the President, Budget of the United States Government, 1986 (Historical Tables).

10. Cited in Address by Donald Regan, Bucknell University, March 22, 1982.

11. Citations are to manuscript submitted by the authors on August 1, 1986, to the Joint Economic Committee.

12. See, House Committee on Ways and Means, Children in Poverty, WMCP: 99-8, 99th Cong., 1st Sess., pp. 157-58 (1985).

13. *Supra* note 11 at p. 69.

14. See, *supra* note 12 at pp. 156-57.

15. *Id.*, p. 125.

16. King v. Smith, 392 U.S. 309 (1968).

17. L. Weitzman, The Divorce Revolution: The Unexpected Social and Economic Consequences for Women and Children in America p. XII (1985).

18. United States Commission on Civil Rights, A Growing Crisis: Disadvantaged Women and Their Children (1983) p. 62.

19. *Supra* note 11 at p. 151.

20. *Id.*, p. 134.

21. *Id.*, p. 136.

22. *Id.*, p. 184.

23. *Id.*, p. 195.

24. *Supra* note 1 at p. 57.

25. *Id.*, p. 54.

26. Gilder, Book Review, Catholicism in Crisis, (June, 1986) p. 34; see also Carlson, Catholicism, Work, and Family Justice in The Family in the Modern World: A Symposium on Pope John Paul II's Familiaris Consortio 17 (C. Anderson & W. Gribbin eds. 1982).

27. *Supra* note 11 at pp. 142-44.

28. Gilder, *supra* note 26.

The U.S. Bishops' Economic Pastoral
by
Regis A. Factor

Since I did not receive Carl Anderson's paper in time I cannot treat it with the care it deserves. But I can state that he has provided a precise and lucid essay incorporating recent studies in public policy which enable a substantial critical assessment of the specific policy proposals in the Bishops' Draft Pastoral Letter. He has described the impact of specific government programs upon the integrity of the family and he rightly emphasizes the fact that government must act to promote the progress of the human family. This essay merits serious examination and reflection. I would like to supplement it with a few comments on other sections of the Third Draft of the Bishops' Economy Pastoral.

After having read the Third Draft more carefully I would like to begin by making reference to a quote that appears in italics near the end of the text (para. 337):

> All the moral principles that govern the just operation of any economic endeavor apply to the Church and its agencies and institutions; indeed the Church should be exemplary.

Among the moral principles, and one which receives a good deal of emphasis, is the requirement of full participation by persons in economic, political, and social institutions. The democratic, self-governing model is the proper structural form for these institutions. What this means is that the Church is being told to democratize itself by granting equal power in the governing of a diocese to each member: the Bishop, the Priest, the layman, and the laywoman. The hierarchical order, with its concentrations of privilege and power, must be displaced. Sexual discrimination is to be abolished. Women have to be given the right to become priests. The all-male hierarchy must be replaced.

We are called to liberate ourselves by seizing political and social power. Spiritual impoverishment is overcome through political activism. One fulfills oneself spiritually by redeeming the political dimension of life. It is fitting that this panel is entitled "Spiritual Renewal and the Reform of Social Institutions," for it reminds us that our spiritual life comes first and is necessary if we want to truly reform our social institutions. Pople John Paul II insists that our primary concern in the domain of work is the subjective dimension, the interior life, not the external or objective dimension, to use his term. It is not so much the objective conditions of the economy which are the primary concern, but the spiritual state of the worker. This distinction does away with the allegedly inherent conflict between labor and capital.

That dispute dissolves along with similar theories of materialism. Labor unions are not engaged in a struggle *against* corporate centers of power and wealth, but are struggling *for* human dignity and eternal salvation. What is needed is not to increase the power of labor by more active political union activity, but to seek the "humanization" of capital. The opposition which appears between labor and capital arises *not from the structure* of the production process.

The Pastoral Draft, however, states that the subjective dimension receives its value from the objective one. Thus the order of priority has mistakenly been reversed.

The conception of the virtues of good citizenship which informs the letter was explicitly identified in the Second Draft with political science professors Michael Walzer of Harvard and Sheldon Wolin of Princeton, and Pope Paul VI. Walzer's and Wolin's names are omitted in the Third Draft in that key footnote, while Pope Paul VI remains. In reality, it is their vision of democratic politics which is crucial in this segment of the document, and especially that of Michael Walzer. For him, citizens are Lockean men pursuing their own self interests. Power must therefore be distributed as broadly as possible, since all men are self-seeking. The Church has always rejected philosophical liberalism. Despite this Walzer continues by writing:

> The most common form of powerlessness in the United States today derives from the dominance of money in the sphere of politics... Without power you have no sense of self and lack self respect.

> The struggle is in itself a denial of powerlessness, an acting out of citizenly virtue; the struggle against the dominance of money... is perhaps the finest contemporary expresson of self respect.

One must obtain power for "the lack of power corrupts absolutely." The democratic citizen finds redemption in the conquest of power. Walzer concludes: "Citizenship, as distinct from salvation, depends upon certain public arrangements." The separation of citizenship from divine matters is complete.

The Bishops' Third Draft is only partly given over to philosophical liberalism. The scriptural discussion in the Draft is outstanding and inspiring, but one is left actually with two versions of citizenship -- the Catholic one and the liberal one. It is not surprising that the specific policy proposals contained in the document receive the sharp criticism which Carl Anderson so ably levies against them.